POLITICAL
SOCIALIZATION

A Study in

the Psychology of Political Behavior

 The Free Press, *New York*

Collier-Macmillan Limited, *London*

Herbert H. Hyman

POLITICAL

SOCIALIZATION

Preface

Now—by 1969—the study of political socialization has become a large-scale enterprise. It has become the organizing principle for scientific meetings and lengthy conferences. Journals devote special issues to the theme. Texts and theoretical works in political science and monographs on the politics of many countries contain chapters on the topic. Scholarship has developed to the point that collections of articles are ready for the press, and the bibliography already runs to dozens of pages. From the perspective of the present, the image of the scientific landscape of the past is bound to be distorted. With this luxuriant scene before our eyes, it is hard to bring back to mind the barren vista of the previous decade.

Then—in 1959—when *Political Socialization* was first published, I could state correctly, by way of introduction: "One seeks far and wide for any extended treatment of political behavior as *learned* behavior, despite the fact that this is patently the case. . . . To inventory studies in psychology and political behavior and to systematize them in terms of a conception of learning is itself a major task but certainly of highest priority."

The form or model that shaped the conception I presented was in terms of a process of political socialization, that particular concept not having been identified explicitly back then, although it is in common use today. That concept then reinstated for me a buried literature from the distant past and unified many fragments of empirical research that constituted the inventory of the evidence in support of the general formulation. And I stated then, by way of conclusion, that "the formulation was intended to remind us of a neglected problem and to provide a systematic framework for inquiry into this problem."

In the present thriving state of inquiry, it is hard to remember that the problem was once neglected. By now, my monograph has realized the prime function intended. That it may continue to serve a function underlies the decision to issue it in a new, paperback edition.

The domain of behavior now being examined empirically for products and processes of political socialization is, obviously, much larger than the realm I explored. The narrower boundaries within which I was confined had to be drawn in terms of the research that existed, which dealt mainly with the United States, and the three dimensions I examined—participation, political orientation, and democratic or authoritarian tendency—had been agreed upon as a common focus by the interdisciplinary team with whom I was working on a more comprehensive political inventory.

New investigators are freer to roam the world, picking whatever country or set of countries strikes their fancy and measuring whatever dimensions of behavior they choose in whatever type of population seems fruitful to them. For those investigators who are now penetrating more deeply into the same realm I explored, the inventory of earlier findings certainly has relevance. And for those whose wanderings take them to new geographical regions and new spheres of behavior, the inventory may facilitate comparisons of the process of political socialization in different societies and with different aspects of behavior. Whatever their focus may be, new investigators may profit from the large inventory of methods that earlier investigators invented by hard labors over half a century. And the methodological complexities that I tried to analyze, notably in studies of intra-family influence and generational change, may reduce the risk of faulty inferences in current inquiry.

Sometimes, it is the odd fate of a concept that it can have *too* successful a career. After it wins scientific acceptance, it may become so appealing and fashionable that it is applied indiscriminately and its sharpness as an intellectual tool is then blunted. To some extent, this has been the history of the concept of political socialization, which today is often used as coextensive with all modes of political learning. The meaning I intended was narrower, more traditional. I hoped to reserve the term for those processes of learning that most members of a society or of a sub-group experience, in contrast with learning that is idiosyncratic in character. The former process produces the regularities, uniformities, that are directly relevant to the stability of political systems and that lend themselves to social and educational policy. The latter process produces endless variability, creates unpredictability, and defies institutional forms of control. The complete treatment of political learning must deal with both processes, but they should be carefully distinguished in order to determine their relative weights and their different political consequences. In this connection, my original statement may not have been altogether clear, but it should serve to recall the distinction.

Political Socialization was originally commissioned as one of a larger series of works, each intended as an inventory of the knowledge accumulated by one or more of the social sciences about a specified problem area. All of the authors struggled long and hard to translate into a reality what at first seemed so simple and straightforward an idea. Chronicles of such difficulties can certainly serve to guide us all toward the scientific goal of codifying knowledge, and this monograph is republished in the service of that endeavor. Apart from minor editorial corrections, the new edition is unchanged with the exception of one small section that has been deleted. The last section of Chapter 3, appearing on pages 63–67 of the former edition, has been omitted since the data were fragmentary and the findings inconclusive.

H. H. H.

Columbia University

Contents

POLITICAL
SOCIALIZATION

An Overview:

Psychological Perspectives

on Politics

The study of politics is the meeting ground for many disciplines. Indeed in the current study of political behavior, sociologists, psychologists, and anthropologists seem to play as central a role as traditional political scientists. Psychological tools of analysis and modes of research are no longer private property, but today have become the common equipment of investigators of diverse formal backgrounds trying to understand politics. Note the widespread use of sample surveys, of inquiries into attitudes and opinions, of experimental designs, and the employment of concepts deriving from motivational theories and psychoanalysis.[1] Even in the ancient writings of political theory, doctrines about the nature of man figure, and eloquent appeals for a revival of psychology in politics are found among the classics of political theory written in the first decades of this century.

All this attests to the vitality of a psychological approach to politics—not as an exclusive approach, but certainly as an essential adjunct to political science. In the service of making psychology most useful in the current study of politics, it seemed desirable to have an inventory of the accumulated knowledge that psychology has already provided of politics. Parallel inventories of sociological and historical knowledge of politics are needed to do justice to the complexity of political behavior and to cast into serviceable form for future inquiry the rich knowledge these disciplines have accumulated. Inspired by this goal, the writer has worked for a number of years as a member of an interdisciplinary team engaged in an inventory of knowledge about political behavior.[2] In this introduction many perspectives that psychologists have brought to bear on politics and the basis for the final choice of one particular formulation for the inventory will be indicated.

Alternative Psychological Perspectives

The long and diverse past of the Psychology of Politics creates a serious obstacle to any such inventory. Psychology is a rich resource but psychological investigators have varied in the concrete political entities they have subjected to study, in the modes of analysis they have chosen and in the methods and procedures they have employed. To put all this diversity in any useable form at all, then to give it unity, to accent what is important, is most difficult. To illustrate the diversity and the difficulty, some psychological approaches to politics that exist in the literature are summarized and illustrated in the following schema. The diversity defies any simple classification but the empirical studies can be given some orderliness in terms of three principles of classification: (a) whether the *subject* of inquiry is drawn from an elite, from the mass or general public, or from some deviant and specialized group, (b) whether the *design* is that of the single case study or involves a series, and (c) what the *empirical base* is—the quality and type of data presented and the procedures employed. With respect to the empirical base the variety is great and no further subclassification seems warranted. Whatever the subject, design, and empirical base may be, investigators still vary in the aspect of behavior they focus on, the dependent variables they seek to describe or explain, and the concepts they introduce for interpretive purposes. A good deal of the early research focused on the motivation of behavior, the goals sought, and was inspired by psychodynamic theories, but the bulk of recent inquiry does not readily fit under any psychological system.

The Study of the Elite

1. THE CASE STUDY OF HISTORICALLY IMPORTANT POLITICAL FIGURES BY REFERENCE TO PSYCHODYNAMIC FACTORS REVEALED IN HISTORICAL MATERIALS. Here the psychological investigator approaches the pinnacle of politics by the direct study of an individual whose actions have changed the course of history. However, source materials are sketchy and intuitive analyses must be made. By way of illustration one might cite Jekels' analysis of Napoleon, Ernest Jones' essay on Louis Bonaparte, or Clark on Lincoln.[3]

3

2. The Case Study of Political Actors with Lesser Roles in History by Reference to Psychodynamic Factors Revealed in Historical Materials. Here the method and problem are the same as in "1" but our distinction is drawn on practical grounds because of the difference in political importance. The distinction, however, points somewhat to politically deviant movements and perhaps principles might be derived inductively for the two classes of political personages. By way of illustration, one might cite Pfister's analysis of Von Zinzendorf, the leader of the Moravian movement, or Lomar's analysis of Loyola and the Jesuit movement, or Abraham and Freud on Amenhotep and the rise of Monotheistic religion.[4]

3. The Study of a Series of Minor Political Actors for Psychodynamic Factors Revealed through Primary Research. Here the goals are the same as in the earlier approaches, but the findings are buttressed through direct evidence derived from larger numbers of contemporary cases. Direct observation and the requirement of a series of cases, of necessity, reduce the importance of the personages. Thus one chooses between the unique study of a Lenin or the study of a series of lesser revolutionaries. By way of illustration one could cite Lasswell's early work on agitators and administrators, or the later work on demagogues by Lowenthal and Guterman.[5] Even here when one can deal with the contemporary scene, it should be noted that there may be serious difficulties in obtaining accurate or complete data.[6]

4. The Study of a Series of Minor Political Actors for Psychological Factors Revealed Indirectly through Biographical Indices. Here the concern is less with depth psychological data, and more with the range of common psychological variables. Many such studies are oriented primarily to sociological concerns, e.g., the class origins of the group, but, insofar as inferences are drawn from biographical indices as to values, motives, cognitive factors, etc. they qualify for inclusion under our schema. An example is Bruce Smith's treatment of the Propaganda Ministers and Heads of State of a variety of countries.[7]

5. INFERENTIAL STUDY OF THE PSYCHOLOGY OF A SERIES OF MINOR POLITICAL ACTORS FROM STATISTICAL RECORDS OF THEIR DECISION BEHAVIOR. Here the goal is the same as in "4" and the approach as in "4" is inferential, but the indices are derived from political *acts* rather than from biographical data. An early example is Eberhart's analysis of the distribution of legislative acts among members of the U. S. House of Representatives or factorial analyses of the acts of the 76th Congress as conducted by Carlson and Harrell or of the acts of the U. S. Supreme Court as conducted by Thurstone and Degan.[8]

All of the approaches thus far cited are concerned with the politics of the elite rather than the mass, the actors rather than the audience. We turn now to a series of contrasted approaches which inquire into psychological factors in the politics of the mass. Here, too, we find much diversity.

The Study of the Mass

1. THE CASE STUDY OF PARTICULAR POLITICAL SYSTEMS VIA DIVERSE DATA SUBJECTED TO SPECULATIVE ANALYSIS IN TERMS OF CHARACTER STRUCTURE. In such approaches the analyst seeks to explain a particular aggregate, for example, Germany or the United States. The distinction between the actor and the audience, the elite and the mass, is not tightly drawn. Rather the notion is that some distinctive psychological structure connects both levels. Such approaches certainly qualify in the study of the politics of the ordinary man, but since historical end products are examined for their psychological meanings, presumably elite levels have contributed to the findings. By way of illustration, one might cite Brickner or Kecskemeti and Leites on Germany, Gorer on Japan or the United States, or Russia, or Erikson on Germany, Russia and the United States.[9]

2. The Case Study of Particular Political Systems by Reference to Empirical Data on Public Opinion or Attitudes. Here the analyst can make use of the great body of data collected by survey methods on samples of a total national population. By way of illustration one might cite Bruner's discussion of American political behavior based on the secondary analysis of a great quantity of survey data, or Almond's later treatment, or Hyman and Sheatsley, or the recent inquiry by Stoetzel of Japanese youth. Here using deeper methods but more restricted coverage, one might locate *The Authoritarian Personality*.[10]

3. Comparative Psychologies of Politics Based on Parallel Public Opinion Data from a Series of Countries. The approach is the same as in "2," but extended over several countries. One might cite McGranahan's comparison of the ideology of German and American youth or the more recent study by Gillespie and Allport among youth of ten different countries, or the comparative surveys among seven European countries."[11]

We have in these two latter approaches the basis for the systematic and comprehensive psychology of the politics of the mass. The approach directly treats mass behavior. It is directed to the psychological underpinnings of political behavior in motivations, cognitions, attitudes, perceptions, and the like. The use of sampling permits generalizations. Moreover, a wealth of data exists for secondary analysis.

The last empirical approach deals with the third type of subject matter:

The Study of Deviant Groups and Social Movements

Here attention is devoted to a rather specialized range of political phenomena, such as transient political groupings in crisis, mob, and similar situations, or deviant movements and their members. The design may involve a single case study or a series of cases. One might cite early work like LeBon's or the series of movements studied by Cantril or Almond's studies of adherents of the Communist Party in a number of countries.[12]

Even all of these approaches do not exhaust the empirical studies in the psychology of politics. Many discrete studies do not easily fit under any of the above rubrics, and many psychological researches which never deal explicitly with strict political content are relevant to an understanding of political behavior. In addition, there is a body of theoretical and speculative writing about psychology and politics which contrasts with the empirical studies. Much of this early speculation antedates scientific psychology, for as already noted, psychology has always figured in political theorizing. Conceptions of the nature of man—his endowment in intellect, his motivation, his affectivity, his modifiability—enter into the writings of Plato, Aristotle, Hobbes, Locke, Comte, Rousseau, Bagehot, Machiavelli, Graham Wallas, Merriam and Lippmann. Turning to modern works which advance systematic theoretical formulations about political behavior, the variety is considerable. Such formulations may incorporate empirical materials or not, may be comparative or not, and may even be predicated on the most narrow empirical settings, but the common feature is that the discussion pertains to genotypical forms of behavior and is couched in terms of great generality. Two different emphases of such formulations should be distinguished. More common is a concern with the psychological *explanation* of mass political behavior. An excellent example would be Riesman's writings. The alternative to explanation is study of the psychological *consequences* of exposure to different types of political situations and institutions. This approach is best illustrated by writings of Lewin and his associates.[13]

The Perspective Selected

To do justice to all these approaches and viewpoints and to inventory the related masses of data far exceeds the competence of any individual. Moreover, such an inventory would obscure more than it clarified, for it would be encyclopedic in length and without form or unity. We need not take as our model for an inventory the card catalogue of the New York Public Library. A useable inventory should be restricted to a relatively narrow range of phenomena, for then it can be brought down to manageable scope. More important, by narrowing the range, one gives some unity and form to the treatment and increases the likelihood that the inventory will establish some valid principles, since all the studies examined have a common problem on which they focus and knowledge may cumulate. By restricting the coverage, there is also opportunity for more detailed presentation of each item in the inventory. Studies are not as standardized as suits. They may vary in the strength of their evidence, and little details may reveal differences in apparently similar findings which then lead to better specification of our knowledge. Such will be our model of an inventory and we shall restrict ourselves to the subject of the political behavior of the mass, rather than the elite or the deviant.

In attempting to bring some order into this sphere, political behavior itself must be given some more definite and specific boundaries. The relatively narrow realm upon which we will concentrate can be conceptualized in terms of three dimensions: *participation* or involvement in politics, and granted the involvement, whether the *goals* of action are towards radical or conservative ends *and* towards democratic or authoritarian forms. The actual materials we shall inventory will be essentially empirical data from discrete studies conducted by psychologists into American political behavior. Even so, unity may be lacking in the inventory. What we seek is the distinctive and systematic contribution that psychological analysis can make to the understanding of political behavior and the presentation of the empirical studies as evidence or support for such a mode of analysis. Wherein lies this distinctive contribution? Politics as such has not traditionally been a central subject matter for psychologists. Thus, if one turns to modern textbooks in *Social* Psychology, where one would expect to find the maximum attention to politics, no systematic statements can be found in the form of chapters or sections explicitly formulating the problems of politics or covering the literature. A simple check of a score of the better known works demonstrates this rule *without exception.* The rule applies to the works of F. Allport, Asch, Bird, Bonner, Coutu, Doob, Faris, the Hartleys, Katz and Schanck, Krech and Crutchfield, Klineberg, Lindesmith and Strauss, Murphy, Murphy and Newcomb, Newcomb, Sargent and Sherif.

This is not to suggest that psychological concepts are irrelevant to the understanding of political behavior, for it is axiomatic that the behavior of humans—political or otherwise— is the proper sphere of psychology. It is rather to suggest that there is no standard or established guide to our formulation. Yet there is guidance if one turns to the fundamental ways in which psychologists have approached *all* forms of behavior. The problems of political behavior can be illuminated by reference to three classic areas which psychologists have always regarded as central in their discipline. These are the areas of *learning, motivation and emotion,* and *perceptual or cognitive processes.* Auxiliary to these areas, one would necessarily treat of *intelligence* as relevant to any discussion of learning and as related to perceptual and cognitive processes. From such a fundamental level of discussion one would come finally to the derivative problems of *mental organization* and of *personality.* The wisdom of this approach remains to be fully demonstrated, but it should be immediately apparent to the reader that most current discussions of psychology and political behavior have neglected some of these classic approaches in their excessive concentration on one limited form of psychological analysis.

The First Inventory

One seeks far and wide for any extended treatment of political behavior as *learned* behavior, despite the fact that this is patently the case.[14] The importance of such a formulation to

understanding the stability of political systems is self-evident—
*humans must learn their political behavior early and well and
persist in it.* Otherwise there would be no regularity—perhaps
even chaos. To inventory studies in psychology and political behavior and to systematize them in terms of a conception of
learning is itself a major task but certainly of highest priority.
This task we have taken upon ourselves. The model used for
the learning of politics will be in terms of Political Socialization
—to be outlined in Chapter Two. While systematic discussions
of learning and politics hardly exist, one is amazed at the extent
of the literature that is relevant to the inventory. Perhaps the
merit of the formulation lies in the very fact that so much
buried and neglected literature can be reincorporated into a
psychology of politics and can be exploited for an understanding
of political behavior.

The inventory of studies in political socialization assumed
such major proportions that parallel inventories of the psychology
of politics from the point of view of concepts of motivation or
emotion and the perceptual and cognitive processes could not
be undertaken by this writer. To delay the publication of the
single inventory for the period of years which it might take to
complete these other inventories seemed a mistake. Accordingly,
the essay on political socialization is presented now as but a modest contribution to the total inventory of psychological studies
into the political behavior of the mass. Since each reader can estimate for himself the value of a formulation of politics as *learned
behavior,* no more need be said on this score. However, the value
of an approach to political behavior in terms of the two other
classic modes of psychological analysis may not be self-evident.

Future Inventories

The next priority would be an inventory and formulation
in terms of perceptual and cognitive processes and the related

areas of intelligence and mental organization. This realm has been neglected in the recent emphasis on motivation and personality as they affect political behavior. What a strange imbalance we find today! Political behavior is seen as determined by all sorts of motivational and emotional factors operating through complicated psychodynamic processes. Certainly such behavior is full of purpose and direction, but it is guided, if only imperfectly, by reason, knowledge, judgment, intelligence. Men are urged to certain ends but the political scene in which they act is perceived and given meaning. Some cognitive map accompanies their movements towards their ends. The role of the cognitive processes must be reinstated as a necessary counterbalance to distorted analyses of political behavior. The exact form which such an inventory would take cannot be elaborated here, but some of the general features and the way in which it would complement the findings on the learning of politics can be suggested.

A central feature of such an inventory would be pure description of the political scene as it is cognitively structured by people. Large amounts of data are available for this purpose of the inventory. By way of illustrating some problems that would be treated, we must foreshadow some of the findings on political socialization. Individuals learn gradually and early their political orientations. This is what provides much of the stability of their adult political behavior. Yet the paradox is that the political scene is full of novelty. How then can the individual have a ready and prepared view on political issues that have not yet arisen? One of the answers is that he is socialized into a party loyalty, and acts in relation to the party's position rather than on the novel issue itself. Much evidence will be presented that such socialization occurs, and the second inventory would complement and strengthen this finding by establishing what a central cognitive structure political party is. Graham Wallas sensed this truth many years ago when he described political party as "the most vigorous attempt which has been made to adapt the form of our political institutions to the actual facts of human nature" for as he pointed out in place of the infinite complexity of the political process, "something is required simpler and more *permanent,* something which can be loved and trusted, and which can be *recognized* at successive elections as being the same thing that was loved and trusted before; and a party is such a thing."[15] Complementing the study of parties as formal organizations or institutions, the systematic description of parties as stable cognitive structures in the experience of individuals is called for.

But there is more in the cognitive structuring of the political scene than merely party. In the essay on socialization, there is much evidence that individuals learn their patterns of political *participation* early. Certainly, this must have some correspondence in a set of beliefs and ideas about the political process itself, about the role of the citizen, about the rules of the political game. Almond's discussion of "political culture," his more specific description of the Anglo-American culture as "saturated with the atmosphere of the market," as a "rational-calculating, bargaining and experimental political culture" implies a cognitive structure which is pervasive among people and which could be systematically documented by the proper inventory of past literature and data.[16]

Cognitive processes underlie political participation and party orientation and give meaning to these aspects of political behavior. But they do not necessarily give correct knowledge of the political scene. The inventory would certainly address itself to the particular question of the relation of intelligence and reason to political behavior. This preoccupied many early studies in the psychology of politics, where some simple and fixed relation was sought between capacities and the particular political ideology espoused. In 1937, Murphy, Murphy and Newcomb summarized many studies correlating various indices of intelligence with attitude. In these studies conducted in the Twenties and Thirties, there was much consistent evidence of a low positive correlation between radicalism and measures of intellectual capacity.[17] These studies would be included in any modern inventory not to assert any simple correspondence between intellect and *radicalism,* but because in conjunction with newer research in later eras they would provide a more sophisticated formulation of the definite relations between intellectual processes and political orientation. One might well formulate as the model of this relationship the notion that intelligence provides the capacity for effective analysis of the current scene and for assimilation of the information in the environment. The particular attitudinal end-product of intelligence then will be a function of the nature of the scene at any point in time and the type of information upon which intelligence can operate. The manifold ways in which intellectual processes influence not simple outcome in attitude, but the whole style of political thinking has recently been demonstrated by Smith, Bruner and White.[18]

Enough has been said to suggest some of the ways an inventory of the relation between cognitive processes and political behavior would be formulated. However, some brief reference might be made to the derivative problem of mental organization, studies of which would figure in the same inventory. If one ponders again the stability of political behavior and the paradox of how early socialization can provide effective orientations toward novel political issues of the future, one is led naturally to evidence about mental organization. If cognitive processes involve *organization* such that one issue is seen as connected to other issues, this would provide another solution to the paradox. Then a novel issue becomes familiar since it is part and parcel of some older issue, and is reacted to on that basis. The validity of this conception is supported by many studies in the generality or specificity of attitudes and a host of studies involving factor analysis of a multiplicity of attitude data.[19]

The inventory on cognitive processes remains unfinished business of high priority for it would order many of the problems in the psychology of political behavior. The third inventory on motivational and emotional proccesses and the derivative problem of personality and politics while just as central to our understanding of political behavior is perhaps less urgent. This approach is currently emphasized; the literature is more familiar ground. This task remains for the more distant future.

Notes

1. For illustrations of all these and other applications of psychology by political scientists, see H. Eulau, S. J. Eldersveld and M. Janowitz, *Political Behavior: A Reader in Theory and Research* (New York: The Free Press, 1956).

2. The other committee members were Richard Hofstadter, Wm. Kornhauser, S. M. Lipset, Chairman, and David B. Truman. The inventory was supported by a grant to the Bureau of Applied Social Research, Columbia University, from the Behavioral Science Division of the Ford Foundation. The writer gratefully acknowledges this support and the many helpful criticisms of the other members of the committee, and especially his indebtedness to Terence Hopkins.

3. L. Jekels, "Der Wendepunkt im Leben Napoleons I," *Imago*, 3, 1914, 313-381; E. Jones, "The Case of Louis Bonaparte, King of Holland," *J. Abnorm. Psychol.*, 1914, pp. 289-301; L. Clark, "A Psychological Study of Abraham Lincoln," *Psychoanal. Rev.*, 8, 1921, 1-21. Many such studies are given brief translations in L. Dooley, "Psychoanalytic Studies of Genius," *Amer. J. Psychol.*, 27, 1916, 363-416 and a summary of this approach is provided by F. Fearing, "Psychological Studies of Historical Personalities," *Psychol. Bull.*, 24, 1927, pp. 421-539.

4. O. Pfister, "The Piety of Count Ludwig von Zinzendorf," *Schriften,* 1910, 8; G. Lomar, *Ignatius Loyola, From Erotic to Saint* (Leipzig, 1913); K. Abraham, "Amenhotep IV," *Imago*, 1, 1912, 334-360; S. Freud, *Moses and Monotheism* (New York: Knopf, 1939).

5. H. Lasswell, *Psychopathology and Politics* (Chicago: University of Chicago Press, 1930); L. Lowenthal and N. Guterman, *Prophets of Deceit* (New York: Harpers, 1949).

6. For a vivid demonstration of this problem, see W. Albig, *Public Opinion* (New York: McGraw, 1939), pp. 108-118.

7. "The Political Communication Specialist of our Times," in B. Smith, H. Lasswell and R. Casey, *Propaganda, Communication and Public Opinion* (Princeton: Princeton University Press, 1946), pp. 31-73. This same work provides an elaborate bibliography of such studies. Also see D. Matthews, *The Social Background of Political Decision Makers* (New York: Doubleday, 1955).

8. J. Eberhart, "Determinants of Legislative Behavior in the U. S.

House of Representatives." *Psychol. Bull.*, 39, 1942, 595 (abstract); H. B. Carlson and W. Harrell, "Voting Groups Among Leading Congressmen Obtained by Means of the Inverted Factor Technique," *J. Soc. Psychol.*, 16, 1942, 51-61; L. Thurstone and J. Degan, "A Factorial Study of the Supreme Court," *Proc. Natl. Acad. Sci.*, 37, 1951, 628-635.

9. R. Brickner, *Is Germany Incurable?* (Philadelphia: Lippincott, 1943); P. Kecskemeti and N. Leites, "Some Psychological Hypotheses on Nazi Germany," *J. Soc. Psychol.*, 26, 1947, 141-183; G. Gorer, "Themes in Japanese Culture," *Trans. N. Y. Acad. Sci.*, 5, 1943, 106-124; G. Gorer and J. Rickman, *The People of Great Russia* (Chanticleer, 1949), G. Gorer, *The American People* (New York: Norton, 1948); E. Erikson, *Childhood and Society* (New York: Norton, 1950), Chaps. 8-10.

10. J. Bruner, *Mandate from the People* (New York: Duell, Sloan, 1944); G. Almond, *The American People and Foreign Policy* (New York: Harcourt, 1950); H. Hyman and P. B. Sheatsley, "The Current Status of American Public Opinion," *National Council for the Social Studies Yearbook,* 21, 1950, 11-34; J. Stoetzel, *Without the Chrysanthemum and the Sword* (New York: Columbia University Press, 1955); T. Adorno, *et al., The Authoritarian Personality* (New York: Harpers, 1950).

11. D. McGranahan, "A Comparison of Social Attitudes Among American and German Youth," *J. Ab. and Soc. Psychol.*, 41, 1946, 245-257; J. Gillespie and G. Allport, *Youth's Outlook on the Future* (Doubleday Papers in Psychology, #15, 1955); a brief report of the seven-country study is presented in "Cross-National Research: A Case Study," *J. Soc. Issues,* Vol. X, #4, 1954.

12. G. LeBon, *The Crowd (London):* Benn, 1896); H. Cantril, *The Psychology of Social Movements* (New York: Wiley, 1941); G. Almond, *The Appeals of Communism* (Princeton: Princeton University Press, 1954).

13. D. Riesman, *et al., The Lonely Crowd* (New Haven: Yale University Press, 1950); a whole series of reports of studies into psychological consequences exist. By way of illustration one might cite, K. Lewin, R. Lippitt and R. White, "Patterns of Aggressive Behavior in Experimentally Created Social Climates," *J. Soc. Psychol.*, 10, 1939, 271-301; J. F. Brown, *Psychology and the Social Order* (New York: McGraw, 1936).

14. In a most provocative paper, Almond introduces as one of his major concepts, the notion of "political culture," which certainly has connotations involving learning. See G. Almond, "Comparative Political Systems," *J. of Politics* 18, 1956, 391-409.

15. G. Wallas, *Human Nature in Politics* (New York: Appleton Croft, 3rd ed., 1920), p. 103. Italics ours.

16. *Op. cit.,* p. 398. For empirical data on the beliefs underlying voting see the discussions of political efficacy and citizen duty in A. Campbell, G. Gurin, and W. Miller, *The Voter Decides* (Evanston: Row Peterson, 1954).

17. G. Murphy, L. Murphy, and T. M. Newcomb, *Experimental Social Psychology* (New York: Harpers, 1937), p. 929 ff.

18. M. B. Smith, J. Bruner, and R. White, *Opinions and Personality* (New York: Wiley, 1956).

19. For early studies into generality-specificity, see Murphy, Murphy, and Newcomb, *Op. Cit.* For a summary of factor analytic studies, see R. J. Williams, "Attitude Dimensions in Public Opinion Questionnaire Materials." Columbia University, Unpublished Dissertation, 1953.

Sub-Group Differentiations in Pre-Adult Life

Political Socialization

2 Regularities in the political behavior of *adult* individuals and stable differences between groups of adults have become a commonplace in social research. Such patterns of behavior may well be interpreted in terms of contemporaneous features present in the adult lives of particular individuals or groups.* But, certainly it is true that the *continuity* of such patterns over time and place suggests that the individual has been *modified* in the

course of his development in such a way that he is likely to exhibit certain persistent behavior apart from transient stimulation in his contemporary environment. One is naturally directed to the area of *learning;* more specifically to the *socialization* of the individual, his learning of social patterns corresponding to his societal positions as mediated through various agencies of society. One searches therefore for psychological studies which will establish the beginnings of political behavior in pre-adult life, the process by which it emerges, and the subsequent changes in the course of further experience. Naturally, in examining the beginning of such political differences in childhood, we shall be treating of phenomena that are only *precursive* forms of politics, for politics as such is the prerogative of adults. In attempting such a formulation, we shall have to search through forgotten and exotic sources, for it is ironical that while studies of socialization and learning are exceedingly prominent in Social Psychology, attention given to *politics as a consequence of socialization* is almost completely lacking. The recent systematic discussion of socialization by Child does not have a single reference to the problem, virtually implying that politics has been treated as an abrupt event of adult life, quite different from other developmental processes that have been studied again and again by investigators.† To emphasize the point even more, one notes in the very investigators who have studied the socialization process for those *social groups* who in adult life exhibit very striking political patterns, the absence of any attention to the childhood experiences that produce such political patterns. Such is the case with writings on socialization among the different classes and on the Negro in America.‡

Political behavior is complex and many different aspects could be examined as outgrowths of socialization. It seems logical to distinguish at least two major realms, sheer involvement or participation in politics and, granted the involvement, the types of political goals or policies sought. While individuals differ certainly in the quantity of their participation and perhaps qualitatively in the kind of political participations, the realm will be treated without further refinement. However, the goals of political action have varied endlessly among people and over time and place. Very little order or agreement would exist among writings about this realm beyond the obvious fact that it must be multi-dimensional. We shall emphasize but two of the many dimensions, the one usually conceived as radicalism-conservatism or politico-economic ideology, hereafter designated as political orientation, the other authoritarian-democratic tendencies. The first could hardly be omitted from our inquiry for it is both central and the center of attention in much of the writing. The second has been given prominence recently and serves well to test the generality of our theory about socialization, for the goals of authoritarian-democratic tendencies seem quite different from those implied by politico-economic orientation. Moreover, our choice is dictated by the fact that other contributors to the inventory have chosen to illuminate these very dimensions, and the interests of continuity in research are best served by maintaining this decision. In many instances, however, the lines between these realms may become blurred because of the emphasis on the generic processes of learning.

With respect to the evidence we shall present, certain prefatory remarks are in order. It is in the very nature of the task, as an inventory of past literature, that the many studies cited will be diverse in contents, in methods employed, in the specific variables of political behavior that are measured, in the specific determinants of behavior that are tested, and in the quality of the findings. Many of these studies may appear to be tangential to the general formulation, and apparently different kinds of studies will often have to be grouped uneasily under the same general headings. This limitation is a condition of any inventory, for the standardization and focus of any new program of primary research on political socialization cannot be expected from hundreds of investigators working independently over the span of half a century on whatever specific topics struck their fancy.

But this condition also has its advantages. The diversity

of method and content will remind us of forgotten ideas that we may profitably recapture in our new researches. The necessity to lump studies of different manifestations of political behavior and of different explanatory factors under the same headings will compel us to higher levels of abstraction in order to find overarching categories under which these differences can be merged. The particular formulation we have followed, fortunately, gives us the privilege of ignoring certain kinds of fine distinctions. Thus, the socialization of children into politics can be established equally well from the study of sex differences or class differences in the political behavior of children. Since regularities in the political behavior of adults have been established in most of the usual social categories, it serves us equally well therefore in demonstrating that there are earlier developmental stages to use interchangeably studies on one or another of these groups. Of course, it is also desirable to point out differences in the socialization process for different groups and under different types of experience, but apart from such refinements all the studies nevertheless bear on the general argument.

Now while some of the manifestations of political behavior may appear rather approximate since they are of necessity only precursors of politics, and the meaning of our abstract categories may have to be stretched on occasion to subsume certain studies, this too has its advantages. In primary research, we might well have one or a few excellent indicators of general categories of political behavior. We might then take a single finding to apply to the whole wide realm of behavior implied by the concept or category. Here, in our inventory, we gain in sampling a great many manifestations of the category and can see whether or not the findings are truly general and uniform for all the manifestations. One of the striking findings of this inquiry will be this very fact that specific aspects of the same general form of political behavior do not always follow uniform laws of development. The implications of this will be reviewed at the appropriate point.

Political Participation

We shall first examine studies at a *single point in time* which establish variations in the behavior of children who differ in their group memberships. These studies do not show directly the learning or socialization process but they imply that the totality of experiences in that childhood status has left its mark and is responsible in part for the adult patterns. Essentially, the studies may be classified into four types depending on whether the indicators of political participation are: choice of ego-ideals, media behavior, level of political knowledge, or responses to direct questions on political involvement and interest.

One turns first to a relatively forgotten realm of work in child psychology around the turn of the century, where differences in the *orientations of children to adult figures* may be used as indicators of the degree of attention to the sphere of politics. In a series of such studies the child's "ego-ideal" was determined by asking him what individual or figure he most admired or would most like to resemble, and by classifying such ideals in terms of their incorporation into politics one may indirectly express the child's likely degree of political participation.[1]

Thus, E. Barnes in a study of 2100 London school children attending lower class schools reports that boys are more likely than girls to pick historic and public figures for their ideal.[2]

Chambers in a parallel study conducted among 1000 boys and girls under 16 in the elementary schools of New Castle, Pennsylvania, obtained the same general findings. Boys are more likely than girls to identify with men of affairs, military figures, ideals in the larger world rather than "acquaintance ideals."[3]

Goddard repeated the same study among 1600 children in Göttingen, Germany, aged 6-14, and again reports that boys are more likely to identify with public figures.[4]

G. Stanley Hall summarizes another German study by Friedrich with parallel results, and comments on studies by Taylor, Young and Hamilton with equivalent findings.[5]

Hill conducted a similar inquiry among 8813 white children in Birmingham, Mobile and Montgomery, Alabama, in grades 2 through 12 in the public schools.[6] At each age level, boys are more likely to pick their ideals from historical and public figures, and girls to pick parents, teachers, or acquaintances out of the immediate environment.

The point is simple but important. We may regard the type of ego-ideal chosen as being a model for the child's conduct and therefore as motivating him in directions congruent with the ideal. Thus already at early ages, boys are directed toward politics and here lie the seeds of the adult differentiations everywhere found in studies of political participation.

More refined analysis of these same studies illuminates certain comparative findings. The sex difference in ideals is less for the United States than for the other countries studied, and in the instance of the German study, sex differences apart, there is among all children less identification with non-family figures as ego-ideals.

Thus far, we have taken as one index of early precursive forms of political participation the type of ego-ideal children choose and find sex differentiations observed in a variety of studies. We turn now to other indices of participation such as the leisure time and media patterns of children. Many early studies establish clear differentiation in behavior which would be indicative of political interest.

Thus as long ago as 1898, Vostrovsky reports on the reading tastes of children. In a study of 1200 children aged 9-19 in Stockton, California, she found that boys were much more likely to read general literature and history, whereas girls tended to read fiction.[7]

Jordan summarized the results of ten inquiries into children's media preferences conducted prior to 1921. He notes that girls read more fiction than boys but less history and biography. In his own investigation of about 3600 school children between ages 9 and 18, he also documents similar findings.[8]

Terman and Lima in 1927 report on the differences in reading habits of boys and girls based on a study of 2000 children. Boys are much more likely to choose literature relating to non-home areas, e.g. science, general information, etc. whereas girls choose home-type literature.[9]

Wall conducted a similar study in England during World War II. 600 children aged 13-17 were studied and it was found that boys were more likely than girls to choose current war news, political features, and lead articles than girls.[10]

Meine reports a similar study of the media behavior of 1200 white children in New Jersey in grades 7-12. He reports "girls markedly less interested in news than are boys . . . on all grade and intelligence levels." He also demonstrates much less *discussion* of news with others among girls.[11]

Brown reports an inquiry conducted among 2500 children in grades 5, 8, 10, and 12 in 1936. Children were asked to check the type of radio program they enjoyed. At each grade level, boys showed more interest than girls in programs of news and politics.[12]

Sterner summarizes many studies of children's preferences for radio, motion picture and printed media and describes an investigation of her own conducted in a New Jersey high school.[13] While the studies are not consistent, sex differences of the type already described appear frequently in these studies and are also documented in her inquiry.

Another crude index of political participation is provided by knowledge of political phenomena. If opportunity and intellectual capacity to absorb such knowledge are equal among different groups of children, it is reasonable to regard differential levels of knowledge as indicative of degrees of involvement.

A study of this type was conducted during the Twenties by Burton. With the aid of a number of collaborators, "an inventory in community civics" was administered to about 8000 American children, most of whom were in the sixth grade. By purposive selection of schools, the sample was intended to cover a wide range of economic levels, ethnic groups, regions and rural-urban residences. Comparisons between the sexes *within* the same schools and social categories equate crudely for opportunity and capacity. If we restrict ourselves to the battery in the inventory with political election content, i.e., knowledge of such concepts as candidate, polling place, political party, ballot, platform, primary election, etc., boys at every grade level from 5th to 9th grade, show consistent superiority in political knowledge.[14]

Data of a similar nature for an older age group are provided by a Fortune Survey conducted on a national sample of high school youth. An information test containing political items was included. Boys were found to be much better informed about politics than girls.[15]

While such indicators may be taken as precursors of political participation, they may appear somewhat approximate to the reader. We turn therefore to a series of studies in which the indicators of political participation are much more directly political in nature. In the work of Remmers and his associates, we have a long continuing series of surveys conducted among samples of about 3000 high school youth, constructed by purposive methods so as to approximate the high school population of the United States. In these studies we find much valuable material bearing on all three areas of political behavior, and we shall return to these data often. For the present, we shall cite some differentiations demonstrated in participation for sub-groups of youth.[16]

In a survey conducted in October, 1952, Remmers reports certain questions on interest in the 1952 presidential election for various groups of children. The data are presented in Table 1. While the sex differences are negligible, the socio-economic differences closely parallel adult findings.

Comparative data for Germany on sex differences in political participation are provided by three surveys conducted in 1953, 1954 and 1955 by the EMNID Institute for Opinion Research.[18] Samples of about 1500 cases representing the population of German youth, aged 15 to 24, living in West Germany, were interviewed. A series of findings based on the pooled samples from the several inquiries document the lesser political participation of girls. One measure is a direct question on interest; the other measures are more approximate.

Table 1. Differential Political Participation in the 1952 Presidential Campaign Among Sub-Groups of High School Youth[17]

"How closely have you been following the political conventions and speeches this year?"

	Per Cent Reporting "Hardly at all"	N
Sex		
Boys	28	1535
Girls	29	1465
Class of Parents		
Mother completed college	16	374
Mother completed only grade school	36	1546
Family income low	42	859
Family income medium	25	1827
Family income high	14	314

Political Orientation

Demonstrations that the left-right ideological cleavage and the Republican vs. Democratic patterns of voting, reported for different adult groups find their correspondence in childhood differences is readily available from other surveys.

Table 2. Sex Differences by Percentage Among German
Youth in Political Interest

	Boys	Girls
Interest in politics	50	23
No opinion on the nature of National Socialism	35	52
No opinion on Hitler's qualities	31	44
No opinion on nature of dialectical materialism	79	85
No knowledge of German government officials	5	13

Remmers in a variety of surveys provides evidence on political
orientation among different sub-groups of youth. In Table 3 below
we present data from his 1952 election study bearing on *youth's*
preference for presidential candidates. Juxtaposed against these data
we present parallel data for *adults* based on the Survey Research
Center's 1952 election study and unpublished material.[19] In evaluating the comparison, the reader must keep in mind unknown
differences in the universes sampled (other than age), and differences in procedure and classification categories. But taken broadly

Table 3. Presidential Preferences in 1952 Among Parallel
Sub-Groups of Youth and Adults[20]

	PER CENT WHO ARE IN FAVOR OF EISENHOWER			
	Purdue Youth Panel		Michigan Adult Survey	
Education of Mother (Youth)				
or Respondent (Adults)				
Grade School	50	(1546)	46	(660)
High School	66	(1089)	55	(712)
College	70	(374)	71	(238)
Place of Residence				
Rural	60	(1213)	58	(248)
Urban (Youth) or cities				
and towns (Adults)	57	(1787)	53	(1366)
Income				
Low (Youth) or under				
$2000 (Adults)	46	(859)	47	(315)
Medium (Youth) or				
$2000-$5000 (Adults)	62	(1827)	50	(852)
High (Youth) or				
over $5000 (Adults)	70	(314)	65	(415)

the findings are so similar that one can conclude that social differentiations in voting preference are almost complete at the pre-adult level.

A similar analysis is presented for the 1956 election based on Remmers' youth data and Michigan adult data.

Table 4. Presidential Preferences in 1956 Among Parallel Sub-Groups of Youth and Adults[21]

| | PER CENT WHO ARE IN FAVOR OF EISENHOWER | | | |
	Purdue Youth Panel		Michigan Adult Survey	
Education of Mother (Youth)				
or Respondent (Adults)				
Grade School	47	(1101)	58	(521)
High School	59	(732)	59	(890)
College	66	(168)	68	(331)
Place of Residence				
Rural	46	(678)	58	(635)
Urban (Youth) or cities				
and towns (Adults)	56	(1319)	62	(1137)
Economic Level				
Low (Youth)	40	(485)	58	(328)
Medium (Youth)	58	(1131)	60	(698)
High (Youth)	58	(383)	63	(614)

Party preference, although highly relevant to our analysis, represents a rather specialized area of orientation. If we take instead the broader realm of ideology, an equivalent demonstration is available. We take only a few selected items from Remmers, all in the area of government control of economic life, because of the availability of comparative data on adults.

The comparative data for American adults can again provide some evidence on the developmental curve for such differentiation in political orientation. Since the data are not exactly comparable we shall treat it textually. In Centers' inquiry in 1945 on a national sample of white adult males, on a question of government ownership of mines, factories and industries, approval was voiced by 33% of unskilled labor as

Table 5. Differing Political Orientations Among High School Youth from Different Classes[22]

| | WHERE MOTHER COMPLETED | | PARENT'S INCOMES THAT ARE | | |
	Grade School	College	Low	Medium	High
Government should have control of railroads and airlines	26%	13%	26%	18%	11%
Basic industries like mining and manufacturing should be owned by government	21	15	21	17	14
Banks and credit mechanism should be run by government	25	20	25	21	22
N	1590	312	840	1862	298

against 11% approval from business, professional and white collar workers.[23] In a question asked by the National Opinion Research Center of a national sample in 1950 on the general issue of whether or not there was too much government control of private industry, 31% of the college educated felt there was too much control, whereas only 18% of the grammar school group felt there was too much control.[24] Clearly, the order of magnitude of the differences is much the same for the youth and for adults.

Equivalent findings covering a wider ideological spectrum are available in other work by Remmers. With respect to the realm of class conflict, e.g., approval and support of unions, the self-interest or class interest of businessmen, and subjective class identification, youth from lower income, less education and families in lower occupational strata differ in the expected direction. The differences approximate about ten percentage points in most cases and rise in the case of class identification to a difference of about 25 percentage points.[25]

An equivalent demonstration of different ideologies among youth coming from families of different social position is available in a study by Centers conducted on a sample of about 1000 high school children in a small Eastern city in 1947.[26] Pro-labor attitudes and approval of "collectivism" were much more characteristic of lower occupational strata.

Roper provides similar evidence from a national survey of high school students. The children of the poorer classes and from lower occupational groups are more favorable to unions, although Roper stresses the degree of pro-union sentiment which even characterizes the wealthier children.[27]

Evidence that class differences in political orientation manifest themselves at even younger ages is available in a 1939 study by Davidson. A group of 102 children, ranging from 9 to 13 years in age, average age of 11, were selected from two specialized New York City schools which served a homogeneous population of superior intelligence (average I.Q. of the sample being 143). Children were divided by income level of family into groups ranging from under $1500 annual income to over $10,000 in income; scores on a variety of social attitudes were examined. The poorer children were significantly more liberal than the wealthy on a majority of the scales, although the exact relationship was curvilinear with the middle income group adopting the most liberal position. Whether socialization of political ideology would occur at such an early age for children of lesser intelligence is doubtful. Very intelligent children might well be quicker to grasp the complexities of politics, particularly under conditions where a specialized curriculum might emphasize political issues. Our discussion below of the lack of an ideological position in ordinary children of this age is relevant (see p. 47).[28]

Authoritarian-Democratic Trends

The psychological study of authoritarian or democratic tendencies can occur at several levels. At the *manifest* level, authoritarian tendencies would involve the endorsement of the principles associated with a particular kind of political process —such as the restriction on civil liberties, the reduction of popular government and the rise of dictatorial power, the mistreatment of minorities, etc. Such tendencies could then be the subject of refined analyses to determine their distribution in given population groups, their other correlates, the underlying learning process, etc.

Historically, one direction such refined analysis has taken has been to see such tendencies, such political attitudes, as reflections of a more underlying personality structure, a more fundamental value system. Thus, in *The Authoritarian Personality*, the most elaborate and distinguished work of this type, the *F scale* involved a series of questions designed to measure *implicit* anti-democratic or fascistic tendencies.[29]

It should be noted that the scale contained little that in the strict *ideological* sense would constitute manifestations of fascism, anti-democracy, or endorsement of political authoritarianism. Instead, it contained items to measure such processes as "projectivity," "superstition and stereotypy," "anti-intraception," "sex," "destructiveness and cynicism," etc. The connections between these levels of personality and political behavior may be posited on the basis of an elaborate *theory* or demonstrated through *empirical* methods.

It is not our intention to deny this connection, but it is our concern to keep the distinction in mind and not to affirm the connection prematurely. If we ignore the distinction and use these two levels interchangeably, as in recent practice, we may not only do injustice to the facts, but will neglect a fundamental problem in the psychology of politics—namely, the connection between personality and politics. Therefore, we shall proceed as follows: In this section we shall present data on the socialization of individuals with respect to attitudes that are *manifest* aspects of political authoritarianism and also with respect to tendencies that have been regarded as the *implicit* or potential basis for authoritarianism. Thus, without prejudging the equivalence of the two realms we shall be sure to have comprehensive empirical data on the developmental aspects of authoritarianism.

We shall treat first the *implicit level* of authoritarianism. A number of studies have established variations in these tendencies among sub-groups of adults—notably that the less educated and lower class are more authoritarian.[30] Therefore, we shall present some data from surveys by Remmers and his associates in which items approximating those used in F-scales were applied to samples of youth. These items are selected for their correspondence to items on which parallel breakdowns exist for national samples of adults. (See Table 6 on the next page.)

Presenting variations in such phenomena for pre-adult groups may appear to the reader somewhat labored for the notion is inherent in the theory that authoritarianism derives from certain patterns of early experience within the family. Nevertheless, we shall present such data for a number of reasons. In the major studies that have been conducted samples of adults have been used. Consequently, there is little *empirical* evidence on the actual end-product: authoritarianism, in children. Moreover, whatever data have been presented on social differences in authoritarianism have been for adults, and there was no explicit formulation in the original work as to the variations to be expected among classes in the kinds of child rearing which would produce authoritarian tendencies. Finally, in certain studies, authoritarianism has been seen as emergent from strains inherent in the structural situation of adults[31] and consequently, the contribution of pre-adult experience remains undocumented.

The data presented thus far are only a small portion of the available youth data. To convey the character of the general findings, we shall summarize them. By inspection, we find at least 12 other questions closely parallel to the contents of the original F-scale.[32] The *differences* obtained for children from educated and uneducated mothers on these items range from 13% in the expected direction down to one difference of 2% in the direction contrary to our hypothesis, and have a median value of 6 percentage points greater authoritarianism among children of the uneducated.

Table 6. "Implicit" Authoritarianism Among Parallel Sub-Groups of Youth and Adults[33]

| | PER CENT ENDORSING PARTICULAR ITEM AMONG SUB-GROUPS | | | |
| | Purdue Youth Panel Where Mothers Completed Grade | | NORC Adult Surveys Respondents Completed Grade | |
	School	College	School	College
(Remmers) There will always be strong groups and weak groups, and it is best that the strong continue to dominate the week (NORC) There are two kinds of people in the world; the weak and the strong	24	16	71	30
(Remmers) Obedience and respect for authority are the most important virtues that children should learn (NORC) The most important thing to teach children is absolute obedience to their parents	83	66	80	35
(Remmers) What this country needs most is a few strong, courageous, tireless leaders in whom the people can put their faith (NORC) Any good leader should be strict with people under him in order to gain their respect	65	63	66	36
N	1546	374	540	217

We turn now to the *manifest* level of authoritarianism. In work on adults it has been established that the less educated and lower class are more intolerant in the civil liberties realm and more prejudiced with respect to the treatment of minorities.[34]

Again, we shall present equivalent data for sub-groups of youth, taken from surveys by Remmers and associates. In Table 7 we juxtapose youth and adult breakdowns. The reader should keep in mind the fact that differences between the two populations may reflect the time period at which the surveys were done, since opinion has been especially volatile in this area. In choosing questions we have, however, tried to keep the time gap between the surveys at a minimum wherever there was a range to choose from in the adult surveys. The youth data are from 1951, and the dates for the adult surveys are indicated.

Table 7. Intolerance of Nonconformity for Parallel Sub-Groups of Youth and Adults[35]

| | PER CENT ENDORSING PROPOSITION AMONG SUB-GROUPS FROM | | | |
| | Purdue Youth Panel Where Mothers Completed | | Adult Data Respondents Completed | |
	Grade School	College	Grade School	College
(Remmers) Communist Party Members[36] should *not* be allowed to speak on the radio (1953 Adult) Communist Party Members[36] should *not* be allowed to speak on the radio	66	64	73	55
(Remmers) Schools should not contrast workings of democracy and communism (1949 Adult) Should not be discussion of Communism in college classes	23	12	28	12
(Remmers) Teachers should be required to sign non-Communist oath (1949 Adult) Communist Party Members should be allowed to teach	66	69	12	27
(Remmers) Government should prohibit some people from making public speeches (1953 Adult) Freedom of speech should be restricted	35	31	26	14

Apart from tolerance of nonconformity, Remmers presents a long battery of items bearing on *traditional constitutional liberties,* e.g., freedom of the press, freedom of religious worship, the right to trial by jury and to be represented by counsel, the issue of unlawful search without warrant, *habeas corpus,* protection against "third degree," the right to withhold testimony on ground of self-incrimination, etc. Examining the series of items for sub-group differences, one can summarize the findings as follows: sex differences are inconsistent in direction, and neglible in magnitude; the South tends to be more intolerant except on religious liberties; differences by parental income or education tend to be moderate but consistent in showing that the youth of better educated and higher income families are more libertarian; urban youth are more liberal.[37]

The findings at the adult level tend to be in agreement: The urban, the better educated, the upper classes, and non-Southern are more tolerant. However, adult women have been found to be moderately but consistently less tolerant.[38]

A number of other questions used by Remmers bear on the total constellation that we might label endorsement of authoritarian vs. democratic principles. In addition to the attitudes on traditional liberties, and tolerance for nonconformists, some items on the *role of the public in governmental decisions* were asked, e.g., the welfare of the state over the individual, the incompetence of the public, etc. Again youth from the South, the less educated and lower income families are more anti-democratic.[39]

One final battery bears on the manifest level of authoritarianism, a series of questions on excessive nationalism, "superpatriotism," ethnocentrism. Again youth from rural areas, the South, the less educated and lower income families are more likely to endorse these principles.[40]

It is clear that in all three areas of inquiry, political participation, political orientation, and authoritarian vs. democratic tendencies, differences among adults have their origins in earlier stages of development. Most of the data thus far presented are for the high school age groups so the general point of origin of these developmental sequences is for the moment hard to establish. However, for political participation, the sex differentiation is observed at a very early age.

When one examines the clarity of findings in the different areas of political behavior, certain distinctions are worthy of note. The adult pattern that seems established in most complete form in earlier life is that of *party affiliation*. The logically congruent area of ideology is less differentiated suggesting that party loyalty because of the simplicity of symbols involved or because of greater direct indoctrination or the lesser range of alternatives available is more readily transmitted in the course of socialization. This argument will be greatly strengthened by other evidence to be presented below. However, the implications are so significant that the finding warrants special emphasis at this point in our treatment. No matter how well individuals were socialized into any particular ideological position in childhood, such a mode of preparation for adult politics would be inadequate. New issues continually emerge on the political scene. Certainly many of these might resemble or fall within some ideological realm on which the individual had earlier been socialized. But many others would be novel, and the adult would have to face them without preparation. However, insofar as the individual had developed an abiding loyalty to some political party, it would constitute an organizing principle for these issues. The party, rather than the inherent connections between new and old issues, would define the correct position. Thus crucial to socialization as a mechanism of preparation for confronting political issues is socialization into party, and this very fact seems borne out by our data.

A paradoxical finding is that authoritarianism conceived as a fundamental constellation at the motivational or *personality* level is least well differentiated among sub-groups of youth. The patterning of manifest authoritarian principles and ideological positions among sub-groups is more completely established. Yet

⸸ the usual view of the problem is that these manifestations are derivative from personality processes established in childhood. The data suggest, to the contrary, that perhaps such "implicit authoritarianism" may emerge from factors present in the experience of *adults* and that ideological aspects of authoritarianism may be transmitted directly, without benefit of fundamental reorganization of the personality.

We turn now to some data on the processes of socialization.

Notes

* Many such findings are summarized in an earlier publication of The Political Inventory. See S. M. Lipset, *et al.*, "The Psychology of Voting: An Analysis of Political Behavior," in G. Lindzey. ed., *Handbook of Social Psychology* (Boston: Addison-Wesley, 1954). II, 1124-1175, and other forthcoming publications of the Inventory.

† I. L. Child, "Socialization," in *Handbook of Social Psychology*, II, ·655-692.

‡ See, for example, A. Davis, *Social Class Influences Upon Learning* (Cambridge: Harvard University Press, 1952); J. Dollard, *Caste and Class in a Southern Town* (New Haven: Yale University Press, 1937); and A. Davis and J. Dollard, *Children of Bondage* (Washington: American Council on Education, 1940).

1. In the modern period a revived use of this technique in the form of a projective question was employed in T. Adorno, *et al.*, *The Authoritarian Personality* (New York: Harpers, 1950), p. 559.

2. E. Barnes, "Children's Ideals," *Ped. Sem.*, 7, 1900, pp. 3-12.

3. W. G. Chambers, "The Evolution of Ideals," *Ped. Sem.*, 10, 1903, pp. 101-143.

4. H. H. Goddard, *Ped Sem.*, 13, 1906, pp. 208-220.

5. G. Stanley Hall, *Adolescence* (New York: Appleton, 1914), Vol. II, Chap. XV.

6. D. S. Hill, "Personification of Ideals by Urban Children," *J. Soc. Psychol.* 1, 1930, pp. 379-392.

7. C. Vostrovsky, "A Study of Children's Reading Tastes," *Ped. Sem.*, 6, 1898-1899, pp. 523-535.

8. A. Jordan, *Children's Interests in Reading*, Teach. Coll. Cont. Educ. #107, 1921.

9. L. Terman and M. Lima, *Children's Reading* (New York: Appleton, 1927).

10. W. D. Wall, "The Newspaper Reading of Adolescents and Adults," *Brit. J. Educ. Psychol.*, 18, 1948, pp. 26-40, 87-104.

11. F. J. Meine, "Radio and the Press among Young People," in P. F. Lazarsfeld and F. Stanton, eds., *Radio Research—1941* (New York: Duell, Sloan and Pearce, 1941), pp. 189-224.

12. F. Brown, *The Sociology of Childhood* (New York: Prentice Hall, 1939), p. 328.

13. A Sterner, *Radio, Motion Picture and Reading Interests,* Teach. Coll. Cont. Educ., #932, 1947.

14. W. H. Burton, *Children's Civic Information 1924-1935* ("Southern California Education Monograph #7," [Los Angeles: University of Southern California Press, 1936]).

15. The Fortune Survey, *Fortune,* 26, 1042, pp. 8-20.

16. We wish to acknowledge the generosity of Prof. H. H. Remmers in making these data available to us.

17. The Purdue Opinion Panel, *Report #33* (Lafayette: Purdue University Division of Educational Reference).

18. R. Frohner, *Wie Stark sind Die Halbstarken?* (Bielefeld: Stackelberg, 1956). The data are taken from Table 67, p. 294; Table 72, p. 305; Table 73, p. 308; Table 74, p. 311; and Table 77, p. 319. No exact Ns are presented in the tables, but from the sample design it is clear that about 51% of each sample of 1500 cases is male.

19. These latter data are combined from Table 5.1 of *The Voter Decides,* by A. Campbell, G. Gurin, and W. Miller (Evanston: Row, Peterson, 1954), pp. 70-73.

20. Michigan unpublished data made available to the author through the kindness of Dr. A. Campbell of the Survey Research Center, University of Michigan. Purdue Youth Panel data made available through the courtesy of *The Chicago Tribune.*

21. *Ibid.*

22. These data are taken from Poll #30, November, 1951.

23. R. Centers, *The Psychology of Social Classes* (Princeton: Princeton University Press, 1949), Table 10, p. 61.

24. Unpublished survey, National Opinion Research Center.

25. Poll #32, May, 1952.

26. R. Centers, "Children of the New Deal: Social Stratification and Adolescent Attitudes," *Int. J. Opinion Attit. Res.,* 4, 1950, pp. 315-335.

27. The Fortune Survey, *Fortune,* 26, 1942, pp. 8-20.

28. H. Davidson, *Personality and Economic Background* (New York: King's Crown, 1943).

29. T. Adorno. *Op. Cit.*

30. H. Hyman and P. B. Sheatsley, in R. Christie and M. Jahoda, eds., *Studies in the Scope and Method of the Authoritarian Personality* (New York: The Free Press, 1954), pp. 50-122; M. Janowitz and D. Marvick, "Authoritarianism and Political Behavior," *Publ. Opin. Quart.,* 17, 1953, pp. 285-201.
It should be noted that the original work reports little in the way of such sub-group correlates of authoritarianism, although the findings

are qualified in the light of the universe sampled. *Op. Cit.,* pp. 265-269.

31. See, for example, Janowitz and Marvick, *Op. Cit.*
32. The questions we chose are: Poll #30, Questions 21, 26, 28, 33 and Poll #33, Questions 35, 37, 39, 41, 42, 43, 44, and 54.
33. The youth data are taken from Purdue Opinion Poll #30, November, 1951. The NORC data are reported in Christie and Jahoda, *Op. Cit.,* p. 94.
34. S. Stouffer, *Communism, Conformity and Civil Liberties* (New York: Doubleday, 1955); H. Hyman and P. B. Sheatsley, "Trends in Public Opinion on Civil Liberties," *J. Soc. Issues,* IX, 1953, pp. 6-16.
35. The youth data are from Public Opinion Poll #30. The number of cases in the grade school group was 1590, in the college group 312. All adult data are from H. Hyman and P. B. Sheatsley, *Op. Cit.*
36. Remmers presents trends data on this issue for October, 1956. At that time, 73% of youth whose mothers had only grade school education opposed Communists on the radio whereas among youth whose mothers had college education, 65% opposed. The finding in this instance is close to the adult findings. See Poll #47.
37. Poll #30.
38. S. Stouffer, *Op. Cit.*
39. Poll #30.
40. Poll #30. In Poll #33, October, 1952 similar findings are obtained. Earlier investigators emphasize the relevance of this component to authoritarian or fascistic sentiments. See, R. Stagner, "Fascist Attitudes," *J. Soc. Psychol.,* 7, 1936, pp. 309-19. Murphy and Likert similarly report this as correlative with prejudice, conservatism, etc. See their *Public Opinion and the Individual* (New York: Harpers, 1938).

Processes Underlying

the Establishment of Particular

Socialization Patterns

3 We shall present data first on growth of these patterns over time, and thereafter turn to evidence on the agencies involved. In a classic formulation many years ago, Gordon Allport suggested that there are four conditions characterizing the formation of attitudes.[1] Attitudes emerge through (1) the accumulation and accretion of experiences, then become more specific through (2) the individuation or differentiation of earlier diffuse attitudes in the face of experience and/or (3) through the occurrence of trauma and/or (4) through adoption directly from parents, teachers, peers and other individuals. We may well use this classic formulation as a model in exploring certain problems. The fourth condition will be treated later under the heading of the agencies of socialization. The three others will be treated now. The model of attitude formation implied under the heading of "trauma" suggests *abrupt* formation at some discrete point in time. By contrast, accretion of experience and individuation suggest more gradual development. While Allport argues the relevance of all four modes of attitudes formation, the data we have presented thus far give greater weight to the formation of political behavior through gradual socialization. Now we shall present more detailed data bearing directly on the problem.

We shall first present evidence from the study of *successive age levels* for youth in the *aggregate,* that is, without regard for the specific sub-groups from which the children come. As will be noted, the data on political orientation have to be handled differently from the data on political participation. Thus, we shall be able to characterize broadly the developmental process although the designs do not work to demonstrate with growth the increased polarization of the behavior of contrasted groups of youth. This method, however, suffers from limitations due to the use of *different* children to establish the features of given stages of development. Consequently, we shall turn ultimately to quantitative data from the *longitudinal study of the same individuals* and qualitative and clinical data on given individuals treated as case studies of political development.

Development of Political Participation with Age

In Remmers' surveys it is possible to describe the developmental process for participation by comparing youth groups in different grades in school. By this means we can establish the sequence for groups ranging in age from about 13 to 18. Because of the well established fact of differential drop-out from school of children of the lower classes and drop-out for other causes, e.g., scholarship, the comparisons are not as well controlled as one would like.[2] However, in certain instances the effect of such a factor on the findings can be inferred and may even make the comparisons more compelling.

In Table 8 we demonstrate a consistent increase in *participation* with year in high school.

Table 8. Differential Interest in the 1952 Presidential Election with Year in School[3]

Grade	Per Cent Who Have Followed Political Campaign "Hardly at All"	N
Nine	35	870
Ten	31	810
Eleven	24	690
Twelve	22	630

It should be noted that, while interest or participation mounts regularly throughout the high school years, interest is considerable even in the youngest group—about age thirteen. We shall have to seek the *origins* of such behavior in other source materials tapping still younger age groups. So that the reader can evaluate the magnitude of these findings on participation or non-participation, we present some equivalent data on adults.

In the Survey Research Center's election study in 1952, an almost identical measure of participation was asked: "Would you say that you have been very much interested, somewhat interested, or not much interested in following the political campaigns so far this year?"

The results for the national sample of adults were as follows:[4]

Very much interested	37%
Somewhat interested	34
Not much interested	28
	100%
	N = 1614

The parallel between youth and adult data is clear.

Comparative data documenting the gradual growth of political interest are available from the EMNID inquiry among German youth.[5] Among those aged 15-18, 27% express interest in politics; among those 18 to 21, 39% express interest; among those 21 to 25, 46% express interest.

Using scores on political knowledge as a crude index of participation, the previously cited study by Burton provides data on developmental processes for earlier age levels.

Scores of about 2500 of the subjects, pupils in the Cincinnati schools, were compared for grades 5 through 9. There was a progressive increase in knowledge, reaching a very high level by grade 9. However, even at grade 5, about age 11, the percent of pupils who scored correctly on the election items ranged from 4%-69% with a median value of 25%.[6]

Using Media Behavior as a crude index of political participation, we can obtain some further data on developmental processes from the study of Meine, alluded to earlier.[7]

Meine presents data on the use of various news' sources for different grades in school. We may take attention to news as a crude indicator of participation. For grades 11-12, 286 news sources are mentioned per 100 respondents, whereas for grades 9-10, 214 sources per 100 respondents are mentioned, whereas for grades 7-8, only 168 sources are mentioned per 100 respondents.

Meine also examines the *specific* newspaper features read at different age levels. As he remarks: "the items where the greatest relative differences are found [with increasing age] are nearly all serious items," such as "foreign news," "local and state political events," "editorials," "national politics," etc. So, too, he notes increased frequency of exposure to newspapers with age.

Parallel data are presented in Brown's early study of radio preferences. Comparing enjoyment of news and political programs for successive grades it is demonstrated that there is a rapid rise in interest between Grades 5 and 8, and thereafter the increase is small. Here again interest develops gradually and relatively early.[8]

Using identification with public figures as an index of involvement with politics, Hill's study provides data on developmental processes. Such identification rises progressively as one goes from age 6 through the high school period.[9]

These findings of gradual growth of political participation with age are confirmed by a large scale comparative study conducted in Sweden by Husen.[10]

A sample of 1000 male youth, aged 16-22 were drawn from the population of applicants for position as volunteer recruits for the Swedish Armed Forces in 1942. A variety of indices of political participation based on media behavior can be examined for successive age levels. In summary form, certain of these data are presented in Table 9 on page 44.

The reader will note that the numbers of cases in the extreme groups, the youngest and oldest age categories, are small and these should be discounted somewhat. Inspecting these indices of participation one notes again the same basic findings as heretofore presented: The beginnings of participation must be sought in relatively early childhood years, for already by age 16, the phenomenon appears to be well formed, and not very disparate from the adult level manifested by the group in their twenties. The growth of participation within these years is gradual and continuous. Taking the groups from 17 to 21 years of age, the increments tend to be small but progressive on these indices. On what is perhaps the most incisive of these

Table 9. Growth of Political Participation with Age Among Male Youth in Sweden[11]

Ages	Per Cent Reading One or More Newspapers Every Day
16-17	92.0
17-18	83.5
18-19	83.8
19-20	83.3
20-21	88.1
Over 21	89.3

	Per Cent Read Editorials
16-17	2.9
17-18	2.6
18-19	3.4
19-20	3.9
20-21	4.4
Over 21	6.7

	Per Cent Who Can Identify The Political Orientation of Their Newspaper
16-17	20.0
17-18	14.2
18-19	16.7
19-20	20.9
20-21	20.0
Over 21	40.0

Table 10. Growth of Membership in Political Organizations with Age for Youth in Sweden[12]

Ages	Per Cent Who Are Members of Political Organizations	N
16-17	4.8	21
17-18	7.2	251
18-19	9.7	185
19-20	13.0	123
20-21	13.3	90
Over 21	11.4	44

approximate measures of political participation, the awareness of the political tone of a communication medium, the findings are the clearest of all.

Husen presents one other datum which is a direct measure of political participation, membership in youth political organizations. The growth of such membership with age is presented in Table 10.

On this most relevant index, the data clearly show a progressive growth of such participation through the teen years. The inversion at ages over 21, may either be a function of the small numbers, or indicative of the fact that political *youth* organizations no longer provide for this older age category to the same degree as they do for the earlier age groups. Again, it should be noted that the youngest are groups are not so disparate from the older ones, indicating that the point of origin of such phenomena must be sought in still earlier years.

Development of Political Orientation with Age

In *heterogeneous* universes, specific political orientations would naturally develop with age in *diverse directions* dependent on the specific factors present in the life of the individual. Thus, in the aggregate any developmental trends in orientation would be obscured if the *content* of the orientation were used as the index. However, what we can substitute for our purposes in studying the development of orientations for a large and heterogeneous aggregate is the formation of any orientation, that is, the presence of some view rather than no view. We shall present varied data of this type from Remmers' surveys using the "don't know" or "undecided" response as an index of the absence of orientation. Selected data are presented in Table 11 on page 46.

Table 11. The Development of Political Orientations as Indicated by the Absence of Views Among Youth of Different Ages[13]

| | PER CENT UNDECIDED AMONG YOUTHS IN GRADES | | | |
	Nine	Ten	Eleven	Twelve
Government should control railroads	17	17	15	11
Mining and manufacturing should be owned by government	16	13	12	11
Banks and credit mechanisms should be run by government	15	14	12	9
Government should abolish rights of inheritance	20	21	16	16
Modern society moved chiefly by desire for profit	30	27	20	18
History essentially involves class conficts	21	18	12	12
Right to strike should be abolished	26	24	18	16
Relative self-interest of businessmen vs. workers	53	52	45	48

It is clear that there is a gradual, increasing absorption of some ideological point of view with progress through high school. In evaluating the magnitude of the "undecided" category, one must have some frame of reference for the adult level. Just as in the case of youth, the size of the "undecided" category among adults varies with the issue posed. However, over a large range of issues, 10% of adult national samples would certainly be a conservative estimate of the size of the category. Thus it is clear that the absorption of political orientation has progressed close to its maximum level by the last year in high school. It is also clear that even in the first year of high school, absorption of an orientation has gone quite far.

Similar findings, on a smaller scale, but for a comparative context are available from a study of a small rural community in Australia. Fifty children of both sexes, having a median age of 11 were studied. A battery of nine ideological issues was used and an "absorption index" was computed, by counting the number of items on which the child expressed a definite view.

In evaluating these data, it should be noted that in contrast with the national data on United States youth, the Australian study dealt with a social setting that was homogeneous with a well defined political atmosphere. Consequently, one might expect an accelerated development of a consistent ideology, because of the lack of cross-currents and ambiguities in the scene. Oeser and Emery express the fact of the increasing absorption with age by computing a coefficient of association which has a value of .45. They note that prior to age 10, absorption is low.

In both the Australian and Remmers data, one notes that variations in the presence or absence of a view are dependent on the ideological area examined. Thus, for example, Oeser and Emery remark that preferences with respect to the distribution of social power among the classes, and with respect to internal group structure, occur at a late stage. Similarly, Remmer's data in Table 11 demonstrate that the area of class conflict also has the highest undecided level. Presumably with additional data, one could establish different developmental rates for given ideological areas.

This finding that different aspects of political orientation develop at different rates, and the earlier finding that different types of authoritarianism develop in different ways, underscore the general point made initially. One of the very virtues of the great diversity of data available for an inventory is that we are prevented from overgeneralizing a specific finding on a specific indicator of a very wide realm of behavior. Our finding of differences in rates and patterns of development may appear paradoxical and seem to require some explanation. But, in reality, it may not call for any involved explanation at all. Upon reflection, why should one expect uniform laws of development or that socialization will proceed in completely packaged form? What might well call for explanation would be the oddity of finding a completely packaged uniform pattern of socialization for many different aspects of political behavior. Our finding only appears paradoxical because we have been victimized by the narrowness of the indicators used in *primary* research on political behavior, by the restriction of most political inquiry to adults, and by the specific conventions of modern methodology. If one contemplates the crazy quilt of institutions, educational and socializing agencies impinging on children at different points in time, each communicating only a piece of the whole constellation of political ideas, it is understandable that the various aspects develop at different points in time and in different ways. Naturally, when one studies adults, at late stages of development, all of the components will already be present and ideology will have had time to become integrated. Horowitz, who conducted one of the classic investigations of development of attitudes in children, within the larger attitude realm whose development has been studied most systematically—race attitudes —reports many instances of different growth curves for different phases of the general attitude. He further demonstrates that these phases become better integrated as the individual ages. To take a cue from his findings, when we deal with adults we are much more likely to accept the model of unitary or generalized attitudes because at that stage of life there is integration. We then deal with a limited number of indicators and we find them scaleable, but we should not assume the appropriateness of this model and methodology for the study of a wide realm of attitude in children.[14]

Comparative data for Swedish youth also establish the gradual development of political orientation with age.[15] Approximately 1000 cases constituting a probability sample of the national population of Swedish youth between the ages of 11 and 29 were asked: "Which do you think is the best party?" The findings are presented in Table 12.

A demonstration of a similar sort is available in Centers' inquiry among youth. A battery or scale of questions was used to study ideology. In giving a score to each person on this scale, the respondent was classified as *"indeterminate"* in his ideology, if his responses to the different items in the scale were not highly consistent in their direction. The magnitude of the "indeterminate" category for different age groups is reported and consti-

Table 12. Development of Political Orientation as Revealed by the Absence of Views Among Swedish Youth

Age	Per Cent Undecided as to Best Party	N
11-12	73	169
13-15	66	172
16-18	55	159
19-21	47	126
22-24	32	141
25-27	35	159

tutes an expression of the growth, not so much of discrete attitudes, but of an organized or coherent point of view. The data presented in Table 13 show an increase in the coherence of orientation, although it should again be noted that even within the youngest age group there is a considerable tendency to have unified points of view.

Table 13. The Development of Coherent Orientations as Related to Age[16]

Ages	Per Cent of Group Falling Into "Indeterminate" Category	N
15 and under	14	165
16	10	297
17	13	345
18	9	128
19 and over	5	79

For reasons which will become clear later, data on the growth of authoritarian-democratic trends with age will be presented in the subsequent discussion of generations.[17]

Notes

1. G. W. Allport, "Attitudes," in C. Murchison, ed., *Handbook of Social Psychology* (Oxford, 1935).
2. For such data, see *A Look Ahead in Secondary Education,* U. S. Office of Education, Bulletin #4, 1954.

3. Poll #33.
4. *Op. Cit.*, p. 34.
5. *Op. Cit.*, p. 294.
6. *Op. Cit.*, p. 257.
7. *Op. Cit.*
8. *Op. Cit.*, p. 328.
9. *Op. Cit.*
10. T. Husen, *Adolescensen* (Uppsala: Almqvist and Wiksells, 1944).
11. Table 39, p. 483; Table 41, p. 485; Table 42, p. 488. The number of cases in the respective groups are 25, 345, 239, 163, 135, 50.
12. *Ibid., Table* 11, p. 282.
13. All questions except the last are taken from Poll #30. The respective numbers are 868, 811, 687, 634. The last question is taken from Poll #32. The respective numbers are 722, 666, 579, 533.
14. O. Oeser and F. Emery, *Social Structure and Personality in a Rural Community* (London: Routledge and Kegan Paul, 1954). E. L. Horowitz. "Race Attitudes," in O. Klineberg, *Characteristics of the American Negro* (New York: Harpers, 1944), pp. 139-247.
15. Svenska Institutet for Opinionsundersakningar, Svensk Ungdom, Stockholm, 1955, p. 21 (mimeo). These data were made available to me through the courtesy of Professor Hans Zetterberg.
16. R. Centers, *Op. Cit.,* taken from his Table 11, p. 331.
17. See p. 104.

Agencies of
Socialization into Politics

4　Foremost among agencies of socialization into politics is the family. Thus, Gillespie and Allport, on the basis of a large scale study of about 2000 youth between the ages of 17 and 22 representing ten different countries, remark:

> "Youth in all nations anchor their documents within a basic family frame. . . . To be sure, the mode of mention differs

in different cultures. . . . But the unquestioned fact remains that the family is the primary social institution in all lands, and our data clearly reflect this cultural universal."[1]

We turn to specific evidence on the problem.

The Family and Political Orientation

A major class of studies which provides evidence on agents of socialization of the individual into politics involve the determination of intra-family correlations in attitude or behavior. When children and their parents are measured *independently* and agreements in political views are established, it supports the inference that *the family* transmits politics to the children. While this might appear obvious, it nevertheless needs careful documentation. Furthermore, the degree of such influence can be established, and by proper comparison of these correlations under varied conditions, for example, for children of different ages, one can establish subtle features of the socialization process. A central difficulty in such studies using heterogeneous populations has to do with the *expected value* of correlations between pairs of *unrelated* individuals, who might be in the same social stratum, place of residence, etc., for this may well be a component of the total agreement found which has nothing to do with intrinsic family influences. In the instance of most of these studies, this factor is impossible to estimate and the absolute magnitudes must be somewhat discounted.[2]

In Chart I, the over-all findings from some of these studies are summarized. Much of the chart is taken directly from Fisher's convenient summary.[3]

These and other studies establish very clearly a family correspondence in views that are relevant to matters of political orientation. Over a great many such correlations from the different studies, the median value approximates .5. The signs, almost without exception are *never negative*. The only negative

Chart I. Past Studies of the Agreement in Politically Politically Relevant Views Among Parents and Children[4]

Study	Sample	Dimension	Findings
Bassett	87 high school children and their parents in a small city in 1948	Likelihood of war	Negative, no significant difference between agreement observed and that to be expected among random pairs of individuals.
Duffy	Freshmen in 1935 at Sarah Lawrence and their parents	Attitude toward war	Correlations were negligible. Author concludes little or no correspondence within family.
Hirschberg and Gilliland	200 college undergraduates and their parents	Attitude toward New Deal, "Fascist Attitudes"	R ranges from .4 to .7 depending on family pair and attitude.
Peterson	Children from grades 7-12. Depending on family pair involved, Ns vary between 45-89	Attitude toward New Deal, Government Ownership	R ranges from .3 to .8 depending on family pair and attitude studied.
Newcomb and Svehla	Children were 14 years or older, N was 548 families	Attitude toward Communism	Ranges from .5 to .6 depending on family pair studied.
Fisher	College students. About 150 pairs of parents and children	Economic Attitudes	Correlations range from .1 to .6 depending on dimension and family pair studied.
Remmers and Weltman	High school youth in rural Indiana and Illinois, 200 families	Political items and Party Preference	Poll items have correlations of about .7. Party preference varies betwen .8 and .9.
Helfant	166 high school seniors and their parents in Teaneck, N.J. around 1950	Attitude toward war, Russia, and international affairs	On war, correlation with father not significantly different from zero, with mother .16; on Russia correlations were respectively .18 and .28; on international relations, correlations were respectively .11 and .27.

Chart I. (continued)   Past Studies of the Agreement in Politically Relevant Views Among Parents and Children[4]

Study	Sample	Dimension	Findings
Stagner	100 college students and their parents in 1936	Ten questions on liberalism and conservatism; Political Party Preference	Correlations were not presented. Plurality of offspring more liberal than parents; considerable number more conservative; daughters much more likely to deviate in liberal direction from mothers than sons from fathers. On Party Preference, agreement with parents is exceedingly high.
Himelhoch	68 Jewish undergraduates at N.Y.U and their parents	California "E" and "F" scales	On ethnocentrism, C was .57. Correlation between parents and offspring on F (Authoritarianism) was not significant.
Morgan and Remmers	Purdue undergraduates and their parents; depending upon pair, N varies from 12 to 17 pairs	Liberalism as measured by Harper's "Social Study" questionnaire	Children are more liberal than their mothers who are more liberal than fathers; Father/child and mother/child correlations are between .6 and .7, while father/mother correlation is less than .4.
Harris, Remmers, and Ellison	Over 300 Purdue undergraduates	Party preference	46% of the men and 54% of the women have same party preference as parents, in 4 out of 5 families the mother and father have the same party preference.

findings bear on the area of war where we might expect the larger social climate to be powerful and these are but two correlations out of a total of perhaps 100. The import is clear. While influence might conceivably flow from child to parent, what is much more likely is that parents are the agents who transmit politically relevant attitudes to their children.[5] The almost complete absence of negative correlations provides considerable evidence *against* the theory that political attitudes are formed *generally* in terms of rebellion and opposition to parents.[6] While positive, the *moderate* magnitude of the correlations, however, leads to the formulation that parents are only one of the many agents of such socialization and that their influence is not that great. One finding in the chart deals with authoritarianism, rather than with political orientation. In contrast to most other findings, the correlation was negligible, underscoring the interpretation presented earlier that authoritarianism may well emerge in adult life for reasons independent of parental factors. Admittedly, the sample is very specialized and many factors of experience may have attenuated an earlier correspondence between parent and offspring in authoritarianism. However, in this same group, parental influence on ethnocentrism shows itself in the C of .57. If the unusual finding on authoritarianism were due to some basic attenuating influence in this sample, one would expect both correlations to be zero.

Any single correlation in one of these studies simply establishes a correspondence between parent and child with respect to a *discrete* attitude. By contrast, our concern is with the socialization of the child on a larger realm of attitudes, since only then would he be equipped with a sufficiently general orientation to cope with the variety of future political issues. The series of studies presented, however, if taken together do establish that such correspondence is achieved not merely for one attitude, but for many attitudes. Whether this more general orientation deriving from the parents is produced piecemeal by imposing one attitude on top of another until a structure is present, or by a more synthetic process of transmission of clusters of attitudes is not clear from most such studies. Two of the studies, however, do shed some light on the problem. Newcomb examines whether parents transmit a cluster effect or pattern of attitudes and finds that this occurs, but is of small magnitude.[7] Helfant also finds little evidence of transmission of clusters of views.[8]

One other finding is worthy of special emphasis. The one study in which intra-family correlations in *party preference* are available yields a median value of .9 in contrast with the usual value of .5 for attitudes. In the Stagner study, the same type of phenomenon is demonstrated. Again, we have suggestive evidence that the socialization of the individual into a *party* is a much more direct process than the socialization of the logically congruent area of ideology. Inquiry is called for into the simplicity of such experienced memberships or the greater intensity of indoctrination or the larger consensus and summation of such influence over both family and wider environment or the lesser number of alternative options. Perhaps it is as West put it: "A man is born into his political party just as he is born into probable future membership in the church of his parents."[9] But we might well add the query, Why then is a man not born equally into the political *ideology* of his parents? West also implies a larger consensus and pressure on this special aspect of political orientation when he notes for Plainville that "changes in politics occur . . . but a change of party breeds suspicion regarding a man's stability of character."

Apart from the causes of the phenomenon, one consequence of socialization into party is worthy of special attention. Mere socialization of the child into a particular attitude or even a cluster of atttiudes is bound to be an inadequate mechanism to provide the individual with a fully prepared view to meet future political issues in adult life. The world is ever changing and the specific events that will emerge in the political arena in future decades cannot all be anticipated. The individual would thus have to face some problems *de novo*. Sometimes, the new issue might be perceived as part of some larger constellation and a prior political orientation might thus apply to it. Principles of perception or cognition and of mental organization thus become important to our formulation.[10] Socialization into party, however, provides another organizing principle for handling the new issues, on which specific socialization had not been possible. Since political parties themselves express stands on many of these issues, the individual simply by being socialized into a party loyalty can adopt its stand on the issue.

The theory that party tie is especially prone to family socialization is strengthened when one notes other empirical data, taken from large scale sample surveys, which also establish the strong influence of the family. These studies suffer from the inherent limitations that the survey has been administered to a sample of adult individuals. Consequently, the measurement of the parents' position is retrospective, and not independent of the subject's or offspring's report and the subject's party affiliation is the contemporaneous adult one rather than the one of his formative years. While the former fact of lack of independence might artificially inflate the value, this latter fact should lead to the reduction of the agreement one would expect for *younger* individuals who have not been exposed to the experiences and counterforces of adult life. Consequently, the findings should be more compelling. In addition, the findings take on new and heightened generality in the light of the scientific sampling of large populations.

In full recognition of the methodological limitations, Campbell, Gurin, and Miller present a unique set of such data for the *national* sample, derived from the 1952 Michigan Study.[11] They stress the virtual absence of systematic data on this important problem of "genetic development of personal identification with political parties." Table 14 reproduced from their work demonstrates the striking correspondence in party between parent and child.

The Michigan findings not only have the virtue of demonstrating our general thesis, but of showing in detail certain subtle aspects of socialization into politics by the family. Up till now, we have treated the family as if it were of necessity, an *in-*

Table 14. Parental Transmission of Party Identification by Per Cent[12]

Party Identification	Both Parents Democrats	Both Parents Republicans	One Democrat, One Republican	One Democrat or Republican, Other Uncertain	Both Parents Shifted	Don't Know About Either	Neither Parent Voted
Strong Democrat	36	7	12	14	11	15	15
Weak Democrat	36	9	32	23	23	21	22
Independent Democrat	10	6	10	13	13	14	14
Independent	3	4	—	10	14	5	15
Independent Republican	3	10	—	10	12	11	7
Weak Republican	6	30	22	12	14	9	9
Strong Republican	6	33	22	15	11	3	3
None, minor party, or not ascertained	—	1	2	3	2	22	15
Total Per Cent	100	100	100	100	100	100	100
Number of cases	657	387	41	102	103	140	59

divisible unity, whereas it may in actuality have a differentiated political structure.[13] Parents may not always agree, and the child may be subjected to a variety of political influences *within* the one family unit. And even where parents agree, the child may still receive *separate,* although cumulative, influences from each parent. The table clearly shows that where the family influences are not solidified, the consequences are different from those instances where both parents reinforce one another.

The earlier academic studies involving the use of intra-family correlations provide evidence in this respect. Using techniques of partial correlation, the agreement between offspring and one parent can be determined, independent of the influence contributed by the other parent.

Newcomb and Svehla present the array of zero-order correlations and then an array of partial correlations. While the contribution of a second parent to the intra-family agreement varies with the attitude studied and the particular parent-child dyad studied, in all cases the magnitude of the partials is less, demonstrating the "additive" structure of parental influences within one family.[14]

The Michigan survey data on the problem are also subject to the difficulty that some of the agreement may represent the larger social influences common even to unrelated individuals, but the writers emphasize as West does that "party attachment, like church preference, may tend to be passed from parent to child and to persist into adult life." Confirmatory survey data are provided by a number of other studies.

Thus in the Havemann and West study of a national sample of college graduates, retrospective data provide a demonstration of the agreement between parental political affiliation and offspring's affiliation. Taking tht entire group, 58% belonged to the same political party as their fathers, and "If we disregard the independents . . . we find that 85% follow the politics of their fathers and that only 15% have switched."[15]

In *The People's Choice* similar findings are reported for a sample of Erie County, Ohio, in the 1940 Presidential election. For about 350 families, the agreement between voter parents and voting children in voting preference was determined by questioning one respondent about the preferences of other family members. For such parent-child pairs, only "one pair in twelve disagreed."[16] As in the instance of the Michigan study, it should be noted that the "children" studied were already adults of voting age, presumably decreasing the intra-family agreement one would find if the children were still pre-adult. Whether the agreement on *specific vote* in a given election, the index used here, tends to be more or less subject to family influences than is general party loyalty is difficult to appraise. At any rate, the agreement is again amazingly high.

Perhaps the earliest demonstration of political resemblance between parents and children is provided by G. Allport.[17] At Dartmouth College 340 undergraduates were queried shortly before the 1928 Presidential Election. A variety of measures of ideology and personality were obtained and the student reported on his father's and his own political preference. Allport notes that "political faith is apparently a faith in their ancestors' faith" since for the entire group 79% expressed a voting preference the same as their father's vote.

Another early demonstration is provided by Newcomb in the course of his study of Bennington College students. In October, 1936, 52 Freshman girls reported their preferences for candidates running in the 1936 Presidential campaign and also reported on their parents' preferences. The marginal distributions are almost identical for the two groups: 62% of the students were Landon supporters and 66% of parents were reported to be Landon supporters.[18]

A similar early demonstration is provided by Fay and Middleton in an inquiry among 575 undergraduates at DePauw University. The sample was predominantly from the Middle West and from the upper middle class. The students reported on the party affiliation of their parents and on their own preferences in the 1932 and 1936 Presidential election. 77% of fathers were Republicans; 68% of the students reported preferences for Landon and Hoover. The marginal distributions are very close with the students showing some minor defections from the Republican ranks.[19]

In another study, we find data on intra-family agreement in politics as determined by retrospective questioning of one respondent. In *The Authoritarian Personality*, the subject reported both his political preference and his father's preference. The tendency for agreement or disagreement to occur was used as an index of a more basic personality factor, submissiveness to parental authority, and then employed in subsequent analyses of the determinants of ideology. However, implicit in these analyses are data permitting us to express the magnitude of parent-child agreement in politics for the sample studied. Since the categories used are somewhat obscure, it is difficult to be certain about this magnitude. At a minimum, 55% of the subjects held the same preferences as their fathers. At a maximum 71% showed agreement.[20]

In the Elmira Panel study conducted during the 1948 Presidential election, the agreement between the respondent's vote and *father's* vote, obtained retrospectively from the respondent, was examined. Among the total group of about 500, the percentage Republican of the two-party vote was 83% for those with Republican fathers, but only 46% for those with Democratic fathers. The difficulty alluded to earlier—that some of the agreement may be a function of common social characteristics of parents and children—is solved in the Elmira analyses by examining father-child agreement within homogeneous class and religious groupings. From these data it can be demonstrated that parental influence operates apart from such factors, and further that these two types of factors (parental and larger common social) may work either additively or in opposition one to the other.[21]

An inquiry by Kornhauser, *et al.*, provides data on the problem and controls, by definition, other social characteristics of the respondent.[22] A probability sample of members of the United Automobile Workers Union, living in the Detroit metropolitan area, was queried as to their 1952 voting behavior and on their father's political party. All of these respondents had been exposed, by virtue of their common union membership, to strong pro-Democratic influences from the union and shared fairly similar residential and occupational influences. Yet among those with Democratic fathers, 84% reported voting for Stevenson while among those with Republican fathers, only 49% voted for Stevenson.

Another study based on sample survey data provides evidence on parent-child agreement in political orientation.

This study involved returns from about 6000 youth averaging 16 years of age and enrolled in the 11th grade in a fairly representative national sampling of schools. The youth reported their own political preference and also that of their parents. There is some ambiguity in the computation of parent-child agreement since certain youth expressed no preference or did not report any preferences for parents. If we include these indeterminate cases in the analysis, we obtain as a conservative measure of agreement the figure of 70% of the total group having the identical party as their parents.[23]

In another inquiry, Maccoby, Matthews, and Morton interviewed a sample of 339 young adults living in Cambridge, Massachusetts, within the age group 21-24 in November, 1952. The youth reported on their own party and candidate preference in the 1952 election and on the preferences of their parents. As in the instance of the other studies, parent-child agreement is very high; "74% of those who can report their fathers' party preference prefer the same party, and 76% choose the same party as their mothers."[24]

Data within the same study confirm the point made earlier, on the basis of data from the Michigan study and *The Authoritarian Personality,* that the family may *not* operate in a *unitary* way as the agency of socialization into politics. In the above figures, which treat each parent as a separate source of influence, generally the other parent's contribution will be to reinforce the view of the parent being examined. However, on occasion some husband-wife disagreement would occur. Consequently the figure of 74% or 76% would be a *maximum* estimate of the agreement when the other parent conflicts. Maccoby then presents specific data when both parents are definitely of the same party. "In 86% of the cases where the parents are both of the same party, son or daughter chooses that party."[25] Thus, the difference of 10 percentage points expresses conservatively the fact that familial influence involves a contribution from each of the parents.

The discussion of the family as a differentiated political structure and the possible contradictory influences brought to bear on the child by the two parents raises the issue of the relative importance of father vs. mother as a socializing influence on politics. The data on the problem are rather scanty and inconsistent.

In The People's Choice, data are presented on resolution of conflicts when husband and wife disagree on their initial vote intention. It is established that agreement "comes about as a result of *male* dominance." Wives show a tendency to talk over the matter with husbands and to be aware of their husbands' opinions. By contrast, husbands rarely reported talking the matter over with their wives. Qualitative data are also presented demonstrating the way particular women defer to their husbands' views.[26] Considering these data in their most specific light, they establish simply the dominance of husband over wife. It would *not* necessarily follow by the same token that the husband *in his role of father* is more influential on the child's politics than the mother. Even if the mother were herself to defer to the father, one would still have to consider the *child's* view of the relative importance of the two parents. However, the authors remark, although no data are presented, that when "the relationships between father and daughter . . . are studied, we find a similar dominance of the male in political matters."[27]

The studies of intra-family correlations in *attitude* provide much opportunity to examine whether *all* children agree more with the mother or the father or whether particular dyads show closer resemblances, e.g., father-daughter, mother-son, etc. These studies are not consistent one with another. However, they certainly do not give support to the finding of *The People's Choice*. The parent that is found to be more influential seems to vary with the investigation and with the attitudinal realm under study.[28]

March reports data from a small scale study of married couples involving the use of an experimental technique and recorded observations of the interactions of husband and wife in the determination of a decision on various political issues.[29] His findings are in support of the Newcomb and Fisher findings. He suggests a "type of sex-specialization" in that the influence of husband vs. wife is a function of the policy area under discussion.

The Rutgers' studies of communication processes among youth provide a datum which is supportive of the Lazarsfeld *et al.* finding.

In Table 15 on page 78, the tendency of youth who discuss politics to direct conversation to the mother or the father was determined. For both sexes and the two age levels studied, the father was the target for such communication much more often than the mother.

Whether the over-all findings on the problem are inconclusive or whether the phenomenon varies for *party* affiliation vs. ideology is hard to say. The former conclusion seems more likely in the light of Maccoby's data:

When the agreement in political affiliation for parent-child is examined, "there is no evidence of the traditional 'father dominance.' . . . There are only 21 instances in the sample in which the father and mother disagree on their choices of political party, but when they do, the young person is slightly more likely (not significantly) to follow the mother's preference than the father's."[30]

The Family and Political Participation

Thus far, we have presented considerable evidence that the individual's political *orientation* is a product of socialization essentially within the family. However, we have presented no evidence on the role of the family in the development of the individual's political *participation*. Data in this area are scanty, but nevertheless provide some support for our general over-all findings on the learning process underlying all forms of political behavior.

One suggestive demonstration in this area is provided by certain evidence in *The People's Choice*. If we take level of *interest* in the election as an index of participation, Lazarsfeld reports that family influences are significant. ". . . level of interest is contagious from one family member to another. Of the men who had a vote intention and great interest in the election, only 30% claimed that their wives did not intend to vote or did not know for whom. For men with less interest, the figure is 52%."[31] The finding again bears strictly on husbands and wives, rather than parental transmission to children. However, it is also stated that similar findings were obtained with respect to children.

The data earlier presented from the Michigan 1952 study (see Table 14 on page 59) provide some additional evidence. Thus, if one examines the last column, one notes that individuals from families where neither parent voted show a correspondingly greater tendency not to form any party attachment. Similarly, individuals who can recall nothing about their parents' political views (which we shall construe as meaning that the political atmosphere was certainly not intense) show a correspondingly great tendency not to form any party attachments.[32]

A study by Anderson may be used in evidence if scores on Chapin's social participation scale are regarded as a legitimate index of *political* participation.[33] Since not only membership and activity in political organizations, but also membership and activity in other types of organizations, is scored as participation, the evidence must be treated as tentative. For 1176 farm families in New York State, such scores were computed for the 2014 individual family members over ten years of age. Intra-family correlations for all possible dyads ranged from .55 to .76. The husband-wife correlation had the highest value. Male offspring showed slightly less resemblance to parents than did female offspring, and for female offspring the agreement with mother was much greater than with father.

The study by Meine where children's media habits were taken as an index of political participation also provides evidence. He demonstrates that such aspects of participation are inculcated by the family. Thus, among families who listen to news events, 67% of their children also listen. However, among families who do not listen to news, only 25% of the children listen.[34]

A study by Stark provides some additional evidence[35] and is suggestive of the subtlety of the process. Comparisons were made between a group of 60 politically active adults, who participated in a Democratic political club, and a group of 60 nonparticipants matched in ideology and other personal characteristics. The respondents reported on the political activity of their parents and siblings. The politically active respondents were significantly more likely to have active fathers, active mothers, and active siblings. The contribution of *both* mother and father again underscores our earlier remarks on the relevance of the *total family structure* to political socialization. A more refined analysis strengthens this position. If an index of a "politically active family" is obtained by scoring respondents as to whether *more than one* member of their family was active, it is found that the active respondents are more likely to have come from families where several members were active. Stark then analyzes this process separately for males and females, and establishes certain differentiated patterns of socialization. The original finding for the aggregate concealed the fact that activity among the male respondents is not significantly related to parental factors. By contrast, among females the contribution of a politically active family environment is significant, but is derived mainly from members of the family other than the father; a finding somewhat parallel to Anderson's above. The sex difference is intriguing but somewhat elusive in the absence of further analysis. It may possibly be accounted for in terms of the greater independence that the male sex role permits with consequent attenuation of parental influence (see pp. 80 ff.). Since the respondents had an average age of 40, it may also be that the larger work environment, which might impinge more on males, would have attenuated parental influence. The different contributions of the two parents to the female offspring are not explainable but certainly argues that the process of socialization into political participation by the family is complex in nature.

Notes

1. J. Gillespie and G. Allport, *Youth's Outlook on the Future* (New York: Doubleday, 1955), p. 8.
2. I am indebted to Raymond Bassett's writing for this formulation and an ingenious formal solution. See "Opinion Differences within the Family," *Publ. Opin. Quart.,* 13, 1949, pp. 118-120. An alternative method for excluding the influence of common *extra-familial* experiences from the agreement obtained is available. Bassett obtains an expected value for unrelated individuals which presumably expresses the net influence of all cultural factors common to the total sample. Newcomb, by computing intra-family correlations separately for more homogeneous sub-groups of individuals, eliminates the influence of

specific other variables which happen to characterize in common parents and children of a given family. Thus, for example, it can be shown from his data that these correlations on the average are *not* reduced when computed separately for families within the same occupational stratum, thus permitting the inference that socio-economic factors are not the uncontrolled source of the intra-family agreement. See for example, such an illustrative table in Murphy, Murphy, and Newcomb, *Experimental Social Psychology* (New York: Harper's, 1937), p. 1005. Another difficulty that may attend such studies is that the children are often used as agents to deliver and collect the questionnaires from the parents. Helfant suggests that those children who fulfill this obligation may constitute a selective group more attached to their parents, and therefore the correlations may be spuriously inflated. (See citation below.)

3. S. C. Fisher, *Relationships in Attitudes, Opinions, and Values among Family Members,* Univ. of Calif. Publ. Culture and Society, Vol. 2, #2, 1948, see especially Table 12, p. 53 and Table 18, p. 76.

4. R. Bassett, *Op Cit.;* S. C. Fisher *ibid.;* G. Hirschberg and A. Gilliland, "Parent-Child Relationships in Attitude," *J. Abnorm. Soc. Psychol.,* 37, 1942, pp. 125-130; T. Newcomb and G. Svehla, "Intra-Family Relationships in Attitude," *Sociom.,* 1, 1937, pp. 180-205; T. D. Peterson, "The Relationship Between Certain Attitudes of Parents and Children," *Bull. 37 Purdue Univ., Studies in Higher Education 31,* Further Studies in Attitudes, Ser. 2, 1936; E. Duffy, "Attitudes of Parents and Daughters Toward War and Toward the Treatment of Criminals," *Psychol. Rec.,* 4, 1941, pp. 366-372; H. H. Remmers and N. Weltman, "Attitude Interrelationships of Youth, Their Parents and Teachers," *J. Soc. Psychol.,* 26, 1947, pp. 61-68; K. Helfant, "Parent Attitudes vs. Adolescent Hostility in the Determination of Adolescent Sociopolitical Attitudes," *Psychol. Monog.,* 66, #13, 1952; R. Stagner, "Trends in Student Political Thought," *Sch. and Soc.,* 44, 1936, p. 602; J. Himelhoch, "Tolerance and Personality Needs," *Amer. Sociol. Rev.,* XV, 1950, pp. 79-88; C. Morgan and H. H. Remmers, "Liberalism and Conservatism of College Students as Affected by the Depression," *Sch. and Soc.,* 41, 1935, 780-784; A. Harris, H. H. Remmers, and C. Ellison, "The Relation between Liberal and Conservative Attitudes in College Students and Other Factors," *J. Soc. Psych.,* 3, 1932, 320-336.

5. For a discussion of this alternative possibility and some methods and data bearing on the reciprocal flow of influence, see Fisher, *Op. Cit.,* p. 37.

6. For additional evidence that rebellion does not account even for such extreme deviance as Communist party membership in the U. S., see G. Almond, *The Appeals of Communism* (Princeton: Princeton University Press, 1954), pp. 221-224. Helfant also provides direct evidence

which is essentially negative. Two tests of the child's hostility or extra-punitiveness were administered and scores were correlated with the three attitude scores. Only 2 of the 6 correlations were significantly different from zero and none of these exceeded the values obtained for the parent-child intercorrelations. *Op. Cit.*

Direct evidence is also provided against the theory by a Purdue Opinion Poll in which a national sample of high school youth were asked with respect to a series of decisions, "whose feelings or opinons would you consider more important: people of your own age, or your parents (or people their age)?" While peers were regarded as more important for such realms as party apparel, clubs to join, and personal grooming, over half the youth regarded parents as more important on matters of politics, whereas only one-fifth regarded their peers as more important. Purdue Opinion Poll #34, 1953.

7. Murphy, Murphy, and Newcomb, *Op. Cit.*, pp. 1035-1037.
8. *Op. Cit.*
9. J. West, *Plainville, U.S.A.* (New York: Columbia Press, 1945), p. 85. See the similar observations reported by the Lynds for Middletown. R. S. Lynd, and H. M. Lynd, *Middletown* (New York: Harcourt, 1929), p. 415.
10. A separate essay on these principles and their relevance to political behavior has been planned as part of the program of the Political Inventory.
11. *Op. Cit.*, pp. 97-107. See the tests made of possible response errors due to retrospection the result of which support the validity of the procedure.
12. *Ibid.* The table is reproduced with minor omissions from Table 7.5, pp. 99.
13. P. F. Lazarsfeld, *et al.* in *The People's Choice* (New York: Columbia Press, 1948), present data supporting the fact that the family is generally homogeneous in political viewpoint. However, this empirical datum was demonstrated for one particular sample in Erie County in 1940. Inspection of the marginal frequencies in the Michigan study for parental party affiliation shows that while difference between husband and wife is characteristic of only a minority of the *national* sample, it is not that rare. Moreover, the theoretical problem still applies whether father and mother cumulate influence or counteract one another.
14. *Op. Cit.* Attempts have been made to infer which particular parents have most influence on children of both sexes, or which sexed child is most prone to influence, or whether particular dyads have closer channels of influence. The data are not thoroughly consistent. For a summary see Fisher, *Op. Cit.*, p. 89.
15. E. Havemann and P. West, *They Went to College* (New York: Harcourt, 1952), p. 117.

16. *Op. Cit.* See p. 141 of the text for the finding and Footnote #5 in the Appendix, p. 172, for some brief treatment of the method employed. The description given is somewhat obscure and the exact methodology is difficult to determine.

17. G. Allport, "The Composition of Political Attitudes," *Amer. J. Sociol.,* 35, 1929-30, pp. 220-238.

18. T. M. Newcomb, *Personality and Social Change* (New York: Dryden Press, 1943), p. 28. Since no cross-tabulation is presented of student preference by parent preference, the finding is not precise evidence. However, Newcomb's detailed analysis of this relationship for subsequent years at Bennington is most relevant to our problem and will be discussed below.

19. P. Fay and W. Middleton, "Certain Factors Related to Liberal and Conservative Attitudes of College Students: II. Father's Political Preference; Presidential Candidates Favored in the 1932 and 1936 Elections," *J. Soc. Psychol.,* 11, 1940, pp. 107-119.

20. T. Adorno, *et al., The Authoritarian Personality* (New York: Harper, 1950). The difficulty in determining the magnitude of such agreement arises from the use of such categories as "blank" on preference. If we interpret the "blanks" as having some substantive meaning for political preference, and include such respondents we arrive at the minimum figure. If we regard such cases as simply representing omissions, on whom we have no data permitting them to be classified politically, we arrive at the maximum figure. In all probability, the latter interpretation is more legitimate. *Ibid.,* Table 14 (V), p. 193, for the raw data used by us.

21. B. Berelson, P. Lazarsfeld, and W. McPhee, *Voting* (Chicago: University of Chicago Press, 1954), Chart XXXVII, p. 89; Chart XXXVIII, p. 90.

22. A. Kornhauser, *et al., When Labor Votes* (New York: University Books, 1956), p. 43.

23. N. Young, F. Mayans, Jr. and B. Corman, "The Political Preferences of Adolescents," *Teachers Coll. Rec.,* 54, 1953, pp. 340-344.

24. E. Maccoby, R. Matthews, and A. Morton, "Youth and Political Change," *Publ. Opin. Quart.,* 18, 1954, pp. 23-39. An interesting demonstration of the consistency of general findings on parent-child agreement is provided by comparing the Cambridge, 1952 finding with the 1948 Elmira findings for the sub-group of voters aged 21-25. In Elmira, the number of cases is very few, about 40. Nevertheless, just as Maccoby found 74% agreement with father, Elmira found "about 75% of the first voters . . . sided with their fathers." *Op. Cit.,* p. 89.

25. *Ibid.,* p. 27.

26. *Op. Cit.,* pp. 141-142. A study conducted many years ago seems to establish this phenomenon as a more generalized one. Moore observed street conversations in New York City and reported that women defer

in the conversational pattern to the male. However comparative study of 200 conversations in London reports the reverse pattern of male deferring to the conversational lead of the women. See, H. T. Moore, "Further Data Concerning Sex Differences," *J. Abnorm. Soc. Psychol.*, 17, 1922, pp. 210-214; C. Landis, "National Differences in Conversations," *J. Abnorm. Soc. Psychol.*, 21, 1927, pp. 354-357.

27. *Op. Cit.*, p. 142. The statement is somewhat obscure and one cannot tell whether it means mother-child agreement was examined and found less significant or simply that *male* father dominates *female* child. Probably the latter is meant if one can judge by the handling of the same problem in the follow-up study of Elmira where mother's preference is not discussed in the chapter on parental transmission.

28. See for example, Fisher's comments on her study and earlier findings, *Op. Cit.*, pp. 87-89, or the illustrative table of such correlations in Murphy, Murphy, and Newcomb, *Op. Cit.*, p. 1004.

29. J. March, "Husband-Wife Interaction Over Political Issues," *Publ. Opin. Quart.*, 17, 1953-54, pp. 461-470.

30. *Op. Cit.*, p. 27.

31. *Op. Cit.*, p. 142.

32. *Op. Cit.*, p. 99. The reader will note that the category denoting the respondent's behavior includes not only "no attachment" but also "minor party" attachment or "not ascertained." However, it is obvious that this is a very small part of the total numbers.

33. W. A. Anderson, "The Family and Individual Social Participation," *Amer. Sociol. Review*, 8, 1943, pp. 420-424.

34. *Op. Cit.*, p. 207.

35. P. Stark, "Some Determinants of Political Activity Among Liberals" (unpublished Doctoral Dissertation, Columbia University, 1957), pp. 28, 42-47.

Political Stability or Change
and the Role of Other Agencies
of Socialization

5 For the area of political orientation and the specific aspect, party affiliation, we have demonstrated the *great* influence of the family on the child's behavior. Moreover, some of the studies cited earlier dealt with adult voters or young voters, who were children only in the special sense of their status relative to their own parents. This, while a limitation for our earlier discussion on pre-adult socialization processes, is an especially telling advantage for our present discussion. These studies must imply that the influence while a *non-adult* has persisted and influenced the child on into his adult life. Given the great and persistent influence, it appears that political life would move in an unchanging course—children mirroring parents, their children mirroring them, and so on into the endless future. There even seems to be other incidental data cited in these same studies which enhance this image.

Thus, *The People's Choice* remarks that "the political homogeneity of the family may extend over several generations. Our panel members were asked, 'Do you consider that your family (parents, grandparents) have always been predominantly Democratic or predominantly Republican?' Fully three-fourths of the respondents with vote intentions in September followed the political lead of their families."[1]

In the Michigan study, wherein it was demonstrated that the parents' party affiliation produced a corresponding party tie in the child, the elaboration of the offsprings' voting history was obtained. From the retrospective report of the individual's *first* vote for the president, it is noted that "three-fourths of the people who report their first vote as going to one or the other of the *two major parties* still associated themselves to some degree with the same party." Other evidence is presented on the constancy of party attachment by asking the individual if he had *ever* thought of himself as having the contrary party tie. The inconstancy over the individual's history ranged for groups varying in strength of party identification from a minimum of zero to a maximum of 30%.[2] For the inconstant group, it is established that this was merely a temporary instability on the part of those Republicans who "strayed into the Roosevelt camp in 1932 and 1936." Individuals were also asked if they had *always* voted for the same party, and it is found that such constancy is true for about two-thirds of the voters.[3]

On the surface, the Erie County Study suggests a kind of never ending belt of parental transmission and a consequent unchanging pattern of politics. Similarly, the Michigan study seems to argue the stability of adult politics starting from roots in family life. But, certainly there is something paradoxical involved, for there has been *political change* as a consequence of voting behavior. We have traced the roots of stability, but where are the sources of instability and change?

First it should be noted that usually we have been examining the growth within *given individuals* of such political sentiments as *party affiliation and ideology*. This level of description is not the same as the level of description which deals with the *aggregate voting behavior* of the electorate in *particular* elections. There are many points of play within this larger system of national voting whereby these stable psychological phenomena could nevertheless lead to political change. These points of play within the larger system and the distinction between the two levels of description go far to resolve the paradox.

1. Lubell has suggested one such factor. Granted that children mirror their families' politics, change could come about through *differential birth rates* occurring within given classes of the population at given points in time and thereby altering the social composition of the electorate at given moments in history. Thus, without denying the psychological stability of the child's politics, Lubell argues that in the period beginning about 1900, there was a greatly expanded group of potential voters from families of immigrants, urban dwellers, and lower socio-economic groups.[4] For example, a measure of differential birth rates for political groups is available in the Michigan 1952 election study. In a special analysis of these data for the sample in Western States, De Grazia reports the number of children in school among parents of given political preferences.[5] Thus, among "strong Democrats," 34% had school age children, whereas among "strong Republicans" only 20% had school age children. Our concern is not with the specific content of Lubell's assertion, which is readily amenable to empirical treatment, but rather with the exemplification of the general argument about the distinction between psychological processes and net results in the political arena.

2. In some of the studies presented earlier, for example, *The People's Choice,* we are dealing with *current interaction*

within the family in the course of a political campaign. Under such conditions, the family's sway over the actual preference for a given *candidate* or its influence on the actual casting of a vote may be considerable. However, the phenomenon that would be of more general significance for our discussion would be the influence on the individual of socialization by a family *no longer present.* This is, after all, the essence of socialization—the *internalization* within the individual of another's views. For such phenomena, the family at best can transmit a *generalized* orientation towards a given party or a given ideology. But, the concrete voting situation involves the interplay of such ideological or party variables and specific reactions to the candidate or to the transient issues of the campaign. Consequently, the parental influences may be as previously described, but yet the emergence of especially strong issue or candidate considerations may attenuate family influence on the vote. While this would not occur frequently, it obviously can and has happened.[6]

3. Apart from the orientation toward a party or a candidate in a specific election, the parental influence is essentially to make a child have a certain *preference,* but whether these preferences are translated into the *overt activity of voting* may be a function of many other considerations. Consequently, political change .may come about through differential patterns of turn-out in particular elections.[7]

4. Where parental patterns of preference are well established, we have documented the transmission to children. But, this is to ignore the frequency of instances where *no clear directives* come from the parents. Then, the child is so-to-speak uncommitted or perhaps committed to be uncommitted. Influences of a variety of other sorts, including transient ones, operating on this group can then be a force for change. We have already alluded to instances where there are differentiated views among husband and wife with a consequent mixed effect on the child. However, inspection of the Michigan data, presented in Table 14 on page 58, which provides unique national estimates, shows that there was a sizeable number of families who provided no partisan socialization into politics; these include families where neither parent voted or where the intensity was so minimal that the child cannot recall the politics of parents. These groups plus

the families with mixed political sentiments comprised over one-quarter of the national sample—a sizeable bloc in the determination of an election.

A related phenomenon is presented in the Maccoby study. Detailed data establish that there is a small minority of families who transmit the clear directive, that they are *not* partisans, but "independents." In the Cambridge sample, this group was less than 10% in magnitude, but it is shown that their children are considerably more likely to become "independents," than children from partisan parents. However, it is also shown that such children are in part drained into the camps of the two parties. (That is, their tendency to be "independents" is not as great as the tendency of Republican or Democratic parents to produce Republican or Democratic children.) Thus, these children are more influenced by other considerations.[8]

5. We documented earlier a phenomenon which may be relevant to the problem of political change. We had observed that parental influence seems to be stronger in the transmission of party loyalty than in the transmission of the logically congruent area of ideology. At that point we dwelt on the possible *explanations* of this differential process, but not on all of its *consequences*. We might suggest—without any present basis in fact—that such a disparity creates some ground for instability in voting or political behavior. If party choice were firmly rooted in an ideological context, it would presumably be better sustained. The fact that an ideology, discrepant from the *actual* and explicit goals of a party which an individual had inherited early in life, is open to other lines of development later in life may ultimately produce a conflict for him and a breakdown of his loyalty to that party.[9]
6. Finally it should be noted that the studies presented earlier all show that a small proportion of children deviate from the views of their parents. This group provides some force for political change, and in close elections could well be crucial. The earlier findings were expressed in percentage or correlational terms and do not convey the *numbers* involved, which is the appropriate calculation in relation to elections. Maccoby conveys this latter logic nicely in the course of her analysis. She observes that the defections from the parental party allegiance are smaller in *proportion* for Democratic

families, but she remarks: "In a Democratic stronghold like Cambridge, there are so many more sets of Democratic than Republican parents, that the small proportion of young people switching from Democratic to Republican party allegiance more than offsets *numerically* the larger proportion of young people switching from the Republican allegiance of their parents into the Democratic party."[10]

The individuals who depart from the patterns of their parents presumably are influenced by *other agencies of socialization* which operate in some systematic way at some points in the child's life. In addition, there may be a host of experiences, reminiscent of the other modes of attitude formation which Allport described, which intrude. Consequently, we turn to such forces and agencies.

As one model for the complex process, we might generally expect parental influence to wane somewhat as the individual grows up. He is widening his experiences and may well confront other groups presenting different norms for political conduct. Of course, these new experiences and agencies may also support the views of parents, but the patterning of life is not that uniform. Interference with the original parental guidance is bound to crop up.[11]

We turn first to the detailed examination of the studies involving intra-family correlations in attitude where certain subtle findings are suggestive of the interaction of parents and other agencies of socialization. Here we should expect the correlations to decline somewhat with age as other groups intrude.

In two of the studies, data are available on the intra-family agreement for children in *different age groups*. We should expect the older children to show less agreement with their parents, because of the wider array of influences they experience with age and independence.

Remmers and Weltman report that the intra-family correlation for children in grades 9-10 is .90 whereas for children in Grades 11-12 it is .79.[12]

Newcomb and Svehla present data for three age groups. These groups all tend to be somewhat on the old side thus minimizing a real gradient of change; the youngest group being 19 or under, the oldest being 24 and over. For the two areas that have political relevance, "war" and "communism," the correlation between parent and child attitude declines slightly with age.[13]

Going back to the early work in child development, one finds evidence from other types of studies in support of the waning influence of parents as other agencies emerge.

Hall reports on an early study which confirms this general picture. About 2000 children were asked what they would do in the instance of a conflict between teachers and parents. Among young children, parental authority was preferred. A marked decline in parental authority began about age eleven and reached its maximum decline about age fifteen. Correspondingly there was an increase in the preference for teacher's authority.[14]

Hill, in his study of identification with adult figures, reports that boys, with age, show a declining identification with parents. However, girls continue to show a considerable idealization of parents.[15]

Havighurst and Taba, using several modern variants on these techniques, report on children's ego-ideals for children living in a small mid-Western city.[16] Comparable data were obtained for a group of ten-year olds and a group of sixteen-year olds. The older group name fewer family figures as ego-ideals. Using different techniques, these investigators also establish the waning influence with age of familial environment on character development. A test of the relations within the family was devised and scores were correlated with ratings of the child's moral traits. Among ten-year olds, the correlations for the different traits ranged from .5 to .8; for thirteen-year olds from .2 to .4; for sixteen-year olds from .2 to .3.

Using media behavior or communication as indicative of these processes, we find considerable evidence in support of the general model.

Meine reports on the tendency of children to discuss news events with family members, peers, and in school. The family remains a high source of discussion throughout all age or grade levels. However, while this agency for discussion of news remains stable, he demonstrates that the *school* and the *peers* become an increasing source of discussion of news with age.[17] Thus, the *relative* importance of parental influence is less.

Burton's early study of the growth of political knowledge provides some evidence on the problem. 255 of the Cincinnati school children were interviewed on their "civic information," and probing of their answers generally revealed the source of their knowledge. These sources were coded under various headings which for our purposes may be dichotomized into home influences vs. other influences, e.g., school, reading, etc. Moving from Grade 5 to Grade 8, the relative influence of the home as a source declines as the influence of the school increases.[18]

These early data on communication about news or political events are confirmed in the course of the large-scale investigations of communication processes among youth now being conducted at Rutgers University.[19]

Table 15. The Increase with Age in Communication about Politics to Peers as Revealed in the Rutgers Panel Study

Among Those Who Discuss Politics, Discuss it With	BOYS		GIRLS	
	1952	1954	1952	1954
Mother	34%	44%	44%	47%
Father	68	68	63	65
Friend in the grade	23	43	23	41
Friend outside the grade	15	26	13	24
N =	(1281)	(1127)	(1397)	(1300)

In the course of a large scale panel study among youth in eight schools in New Jersey the tendency of the child to discuss politics with particular other individuals, father, mother, or peers, was determined. The data presented in Table 15 were obtained from children in the 9th and 10th grades in 1952, and again from these same children two years later when they were in the 11th and 12th grades. They show that political discussion *as such* increases with age, but the direction of such discussion increasingly goes to peers rather than to parents. While discussion with parents does not decline in *absolute* terms, its magnitude *relative* to other sources does decline. Other data in these studies show that this is part of a general tendency for communication on all topics to flow to peers with age, and politics is simply carried along with the general trend.

Additional evidence in support of this model is available from the Elmira study.

The agreement between father's political preference and child's vote in 1948 is presented separately for various age groups of voters. By contrast with the data presented thus far, all these individuals are adult and subject to a greater flux of experience than the age groups just described. However, in another perspective, it is clear that the young voters, 21–25, have had less possibility of diverse experiences than the voters in older age groups, e.g., 35–44 or 45 and over. The data show a *progressive and continuous reduction* in parent-child agreement for each successive age group.[20]

Newcomb's Bennington study provides a similar demonstration. It will be recalled that the student reported on her own preference in the 1936 Presidential election and on the parents' preferences. Comparisons were made of the distributions of parent and daughter preferences for freshman vs. sophomore vs. junior and senior years to determine the influence of the relatively homogeneous Bennington environment which intervened during these years. The findings demonstrate that the distribution of student preferences, almost identical with parent preferences during the first year of college, diverges considerably from parent preferences by the sophomore year and becomes markedly different by the senior year.[21]

The studies of intra-family agreement in attitude provide one other type of evidence which inferentially supports our notion of the attenuation of parental influence as the child comes into contact with new groups through age and independence.

In these studies, the agreement in views between siblings is sometimes determined. If parental political environment were the sole source, one would expect siblings to show a high resemblance.

Newcomb in summarizing such data indicates that the agreements are only moderate and in some instances rather low. He notes the factors of age or sex of the two siblings do not seem important, and concludes that the differential absorption of views must therefore be due in part to "personality differences, including child-parent and sibling relationships" and to "those complicated chains of events which result in different circles of acquaintances and different spheres of influence among members of the same family."[22]

We shall return later to personality factors as they mediate these more general processes. For the moment we wish to emphasize the second conclusion that siblings, sharing the same familial influences, nevertheless, diverge presumably because other sources of influence are not shared in common by them.

In line with our general model, we might also expect certain sex differences in these growth processes. Age presumably brings freedom and independence with consequent opportunity to orient oneself to others besides parents. We shall assume that the male sex role permits greater independence and conceivably the attentuation of the parental influence on politics should be greater.

In the study of a national sample of college graduates, it was demonstrated that a small proportion of the graduates deviated from the politics of their parents. In examining these defections, which came mainly from Democratic families, it is established that sons defected much more frequently than daughters.[23]

In the studies of intra-family agreement in attitude, the findings, while not conclusive in all studies, show a consistent pattern. Fisher and Newcomb and Svehla report that daughters resemble parents attitudinally more than sons do.[24]

In *The People's Choice,* respondents were asked where they obtained most of the information or impressions that were responsible for the formation of their vote. Impersonal sources such as media were studied, but among human agents of influence, three types were analyzed, "relatives," "business contacts," and "friends or neighbors." When the relative influence of these three agencies is examined, it is very clear that men are essentially influenced by business contacts whereas women report influence predominantly from relatives. While these data refer to adult voters participating in the election, we may legitimately regard this adult pattern as expressive of a more general process, consistent with our other data, in which women would be more exclusively subject to the socialization influence of family.[25]

Comparative data from England are available for a panel study conducted during the General Election of 1950 on a sample of the electorate of Greenwich.[26] Women discussed politics with family members much more often than with friends or co-workers. Men by contrast direct discussion mainly to co-workers and thereafter equally to friends or family members.

In Elmira similar sex differences are obtained. Respondents were asked with whom they had discussed politics and to whom they would go to discuss a political question. Married women were more prone to mention a family member than were married men.[27]

Reëxamination of the findings of the Rileys for sex differences (see Table 15, page 78) gives some small confirmation of the point we are making about sex differences. The changes in direction of communication were presented separately for boys and girls, and it was to be noted that the magnitude of change in the direction of *peers* is about the same for both sexes. It is to be noted, however, that boys at the *younger* age level do not direct their political communications to mothers as much as girls do.

From these many different strands, we see that the *relative* influence of parental norms declines as peers and other agencies exert their influence on the growing individual. The consequences of this process in a summary form may be seen in other data collected by Maccoby.

She obtained agreement in political party affiliation between the young voter and three other non-parent groups, friends, fellow-workers, and spouse. "Seventy-seven per cent of the married young voters had the same party preference as their spouses; 64% had the same party preference as the majority of their friends, and 46% of those who worked agreed in party choice with the majority of their fellow-workers."[28] As is pointed out, these figures probably reflect two processes, the choice of like-minded individuals by the respondent and their actual influence on his views. It is clear, however, from the juxtaposition of these findings with her findings on parent-child agreement that the parental source is still the most powerful at this stage of life.

The Elmira data provide several findings parallel to the Maccoby findings.

First, if we examine the young age group, 21–25, for the agreement between the respondent's vote and the vote of the three close friends, agreement is obtained in 53% of the cases. Elmira documents the fact that such friend-respondent mutual agreement *increases with age.* Whether this represents the opportunity with time for the individual to iron out the inconsistencies in his social life and to form stable associations with like-minded individuals, or the concurrent operation of the fact (previously documented) that the younger individual is relatively more bound to parents than to other groupings or both processes is hard to say.[29]

While the Elmira data support the Cambridge data on the lesser significance of friends, the findings on spouses' influence differ. An analysis is presented of the voting preferences of respondents from given parental political traditions, now married to individuals of given political views. Thus it is possible to determine whether the parental family pattern overrides the contemporary (conjugal) family's influence. "Voting is adjusted in the contemporary group at the expense of parents."[30]

Again, the difference between the two sets of findings may well be a function of the age levels studied. It seems thoroughly plausible among older individuals, *married for long periods of time,* that the contemporary family would assert itself over a long gone parental influence. By contrast, the Cambridge study must have dealt with a relatively newly married group perhaps still dominated by parental ties.

An equivalent demonstration of the relative influence of parents vs. others is available for the realm of ideology from one study using intra-family correlations.

In the Remmers and Weltman study, the correlation in ideology for the parent-child pair was .86. The parallel correlation was computed for the teacher-child pair and the value obtained was .65.[31]

Another demonstration in the ideological realm is provided by the classic studies in The Character Education Inquiry. While the specific dimension is that of moral values, the data are included because of their almost unique features.

In 1925 over one thousand children in the fifth through ninth grades in a number of small suburban towns and one small city were given a test of "moral knowledge." The same test was administered independently to a variety of other individuals regarded as the sources of the child's values, parents, public-school teachers, Sunday School teachers, etc. On the basis of a sociometric type of question on friendship, the best friends (already administered the test) could be examined as another source of influence. The correlations between children's values and the values of these other possible sources of influence, presented in Table 16 express the hierarchy of influence.[32] It can be seen that for these *young* children the parents far outweigh other parties as agents of socialization.

Table 16. Resemblances in Moral Knowledge Between Children and Various Agents of Socialization as Obtained by the Character Education Inquiry

Agent of Socialization	Correlation	N
Parents	.55	416
Friends	.35	1020
Club leaders	.14	204
Public-school teachers	.06	695
Sunday School teachers	.002	205

Table 17. Increased Resemblance in Moral Values Between Child and Peers with Age[33]

Grade	Correlation	N
9	.25	181
8	.21	237
7	.23	328
6	.05	157
5	.15	168

Relevant to our earlier discussion of the differentiated structure of the family and variations in influence of parents, Hartshorne and May analyze the resemblance of child to mother vs. father, when the other parent's influence is excluded. The partial "r" for mother-child resemblance is much higher than for father.

While the influence of peers is small for the group in the aggregate, Hartshorne and May show that peer influence, following our model, increases with age. The data are presented in Table 17 on the previous page.

Participation and Other
Agencies of Socialization

Our discussion of the rise of other agencies of socialization has thus far been in terms of the political *orientations* that are transmitted. These different agencies might also transmit norms with respect to sheer political *participation*. One datum in the Rutgers' study is relevant.[34] The influence from peers in the course of development was hypothesized as operating in the direction of norms of *youth culture,* which has generally been identified with irresponsibility and the repudiation of adult roles. Consequently, a small sample of high school youth were classified on the basis of a number of special measures into the categories: "parent-oriented" vs. "peer oriented." In conformity with the hypothesis, it was found that the "peer oriented" youth were less interested in politics, and less desirous of being interested.

Individual Differences and
Agencies of Socialization

Thus far we have suggested certain other agencies which would probably intervene generally in the development of *most individuals* and which would attenuate the influence of the family on the child's politics. We turn now to other experiences occurring more capriciously in the lives of particular or occasional individuals and influencing their political development.

1. SOCIAL MOBILITY:

By virtue of mobility, some individuals would confront groups and experiences quite different in character from those in their parental milieu and changes in political orientation might occur. A number of studies give support to this view.

Havemann and West present data on the party identification of a large national sample of college graduates. As previously noted, these individuals follow closely the political orientation of their families. However, among *the small group* who change, the shift appears related to social mobility. Among those graduates who came from Democratic families, the proportion who themselves are Democrats declines markedly in the higher income brackets. However, among individuals of Republican origins, low income does not alter their Republican orientation.[35]

These data suggest that only *upward* mobility produces an attenuation of parental influence, and appear interpretable not so much in terms of new group membership and the corresponding experiences, but in terms of *reference group* concepts. The upward mobile person gladly absorbs the norms of the new group, but those who move down maintain their former reference groups; they cling to the values of the former and more prestigious group. The Havemann and West finding for adult college graduates is confirmed in the Maccoby study.

Within the sample of Cambridge youth, groups were identified as non-mobile, upward-mobile, and downward-mobile on the basis of the relationship between father's job and child's job. The upward mobile approximate the party identification of their new group, whereas, the downward mobile maintain the party identification of the class from which they originated.[36] One contradiction occurs between these two studies. In the Havemann and West study, the defections from the Democratic party among the upward mobile tended to flow into the category of "independent voters" among the younger group of graduates (those under 40). It is as if in the rejection of the parents' influence, the individual finds it difficult to cross all the way over into the ranks of the other party. By contrast, in the Maccoby study which dealt with the age group 21–24, there was a striking tendency for the upward mobile youth to identify with the opposite party, and *not* to identify themselves as "independents."

The Elmira study also demonstrates the influence of mobility in attenuating parental influence on the child's vote. The analysis is limited essentially to *upwardly* mobile children, but it establishes, for example, the fact that upwardly mobile children from Democratic parents are more likely to become Republican than those who have not been mobile.[37] The data of the Maccoby study and the Elmira study are not presented in ways sufficiently comparable to make precise comparisons. However, it *appears* that the influence of mobility in altering preference is much greater in the Cambridge youth than in the total group examined in Elmira. The finding is intriguing and warrants some tentative explanation. One might conjecture that the upward mobile *youth* is just beginning his ascent, and that his horizon is perhaps limitless with consequences for his politics. By contrast, this particular Elmira analysis includes individuals of *all age levels* and perhaps many whose transit has been terminated or aborted, with consequent attenuating influences on their move into the Republican ranks.[38] Or perhaps the difference may be a function of a more general psychological tendency of youth to be less bound by tradition and habit and sentiment than older people.

2. Geographical Mobility:

We have documented the fact that children moving into higher strata than their parents may break from the Democratic political tradition of their parents. In part, this reflects their assumption of a new reference group and in part is the consequence of new experience. By the same token, geographical mobility would often bring a child into a new political world and thereby attenuate parental influence. Earlier the fact was noted that some of the parent-child resemblance observed in many studies may reflect the common social characteristics and corollary experiences they share. But in addition, the larger environment of the individual, if stable, would generally not conflict with the views of parents. We need only think for example, of residence in the South as illustrative of the latter situation. The Southern child absorbing Democratic party ties from his parents finds them confirmed by his larger environment, and by the other agencies of socialization into politics.[39] Now, if such an individual at some stage in his development moved to a Northern and Republican community, he would confront many agencies and experiences which might attenuate his historic party preference.[40] We find only one study which *directly* examines this effect of mobility, but the Elmira and Cambridge study inferentially support this argument.

In the study of the national sample of college graduates, the party affiliations of four groups of graduates were examined: nonmobile graduates reared and remaining in either the North or the South, and geographically mobile graduates reared in South or North who have moved to the other region. While the geographically mobile depart from the political pattern exhibited by the stationary graduates, they do not approximate the politics of the region into which they have moved. Similar to the finding reported above for social mobility, movement from South to North produces more departure from the Democratic pattern traditional for Southerners than movement from North to South produces departure from traditional Republican ties. If we examine the specific influences of geographical mobility from South to North in producing defection from father's politics, it is observed that 73% of stationary Southerners maintain their father's politics, in contrast to the 52% for Southerners who have moved North.[41]

Elmira and Cambridge are communities of a predominant political tone, respectively Republican and Democratic. If the predominant influence of an area can attenuate the parental influence, we should expect parent-child resemblance to be less for Democrats in Elmira, and less for Republicans in Cambridge.[42]

In Cambridge, 81% of respondents from Democratic fathers

are Democratic, whereas among Republican fathers, the figure is 60%.[43] In Elmira, by contrast, among the comparable age group (21–25), of those with Republican fathers 82% voted Republican in 1948 but of those with Democratic fathers only 67% voted Democratic.[44] The larger political atmosphere attenuates parental influence for *that group that is deviant or in the minority*. The underpinnings of the process may be seen even better if we contrast the findings of the two studies on the resemblances of respondents to other socialization agents—their friends and co-workers. As both studies remark, volition no doubt enters into patterns of association,

Table 18. The Political Resemblance of Friends and Co-Workers as Related to the General Political Complexion of the Community[46]

CAMBRIDGE

	YOUNG VOTERS WHO ARE	
	Republican	Democratic
Friends Mostly		
Republican	52	12
Democratic	28	74
Independent or 50-50	20	14
N =	71	203
Co-Workers Mostly		
Republican	35	27
Democratic	42	52
Independent or 50-50	23	21
N =	48	132

ELMIRA

	VOTERS WHO ARE	
	Republican	Democratic
Three Friends		
All Republican	55	9
All Democratic	3	47
Other Combinations	42	44
N =	481	191
Three Co-Workers		
All Republican	45	10
All Democratic	4	28
Other Combinations	51	62
N =	224	138

and individuals are eager to find like-minded individuals. But volition applies equally well to Democratic and Republican partisans.
Volition apart, in Elmira, it would be harder for an individual to
find Democratic associates, whereas in Cambridge, it would be
harder to find Republican associates. Thus, the *minority* individual
would obtain less reinforcement for his parental pattern in the new
primary group ties he could develop. The detailed data are presented in Table 18 summarized from the two studies. Inferentially,
the Kornhauser study of Detroit automobile workers is suggestive of
a similar process.[45] In 1952, the automobile worker of Republican
parents was exposed to predominantly pro-Democratic influences
from his co-workers, official Democratic support by the union, and
the predominantly Democratic atmosphere of the city of Detroit.
Now if parental influences were not attenuated by such counter
forces, the transmission from parent to offspring should be equal
in magnitude for Republican and Democratic parents. Yet 84% of
the Democratic fathers produced a Democratic, but only 51% of
Republican fathers transmitted a Republican vote.

3. REBELLION AND THE ATTENUATION OF PARENTAL INFLUENCES:
We earlier suggested as a model for the development of political views that with age and new experience, most children
gradually grow away from *exclusive* attachment to parents and
take on the political complexion of other groups; friends, teachers, co-workers, and wives. Such new agencies and their inter-
vention should be regarded as a normal state of affairs but in
the United States their operation normally is *not polar* to that
of parents. Considerable data have been presented to show, for
example, that despite the presence of such groups youth still
are oriented to parents—perhaps even more strongly than to
other groups. Moreover, all these groups may hold a common
political orientation so that no conflict or opposition is felt, or
the individual so selects them that no conflicts occur.[47] Finally,
considerable evidence has been reported that *negative* correlations are a great rarity in the many studies of intra-family resemblance in attitude, strongly suggesting that *most* children do
not manifest rebellion against parents in the form of taking on

an opposing view of politics. However, *in a small number of instances*, it may be the case that rebellion from parents is intense and manifests itself along political lines.

Data on the problem are provided by Maccoby for the Cambridge study. One indirect measure of such rebellion is provided by a question on the amount of parental control exercised over the youth; the assumption being that the greater control would produce greater impulse to rebel. Such strictness of control was related to an "index of political change by young voter" from the parental views, and the data, in somewhat abbreviated form are presented in Table 19.

Table 19. The Relation of Strictness of Parental Control to Political Change from Parents' Views Among Cambridge Youth[48]

| | PARENTS HAD | | |
Young Voter Showed	Lot to Say	About Average Amount	Left Respondent Alone
Change toward Republican	32%	17%	26%
No change	50	69	56
Change toward Democrat	18	14	18
N =	74	69	140

Highest conformity to parents, politics occurs for the group where control was moderate. For those individuals who have been left free, conformity to parents' politics is less, but it is least among that group who were subject to strictest control and presumably felt most rebellious. A number of more refined conclusions are reported. Maccoby remarks that the influence of parental strictness is greatest in those instances where the parents have strong political interests, implying that when politics is not important "children will choose some other area in which to signify their loyalty or protest."

In addition, as the reader can also note in the table the rebellion manifests itself in the direction of increasing Republican ties. These two findings suggest some qualification on any over-simple view of the problem. Thus, rebellion may not manifest itself in political channels, and contrary to traditional views, its manifestation does *not* necessarily go into *radical* directions. As Maccoby remarks, since the strictly controlled youth came from lower economic levels mainly, and since Cambridge parents generally were more likely to be Democratic, such rebellion from parental views must, of necessity, go in the direction of the Republicans. The motivation may be to change, but the *direction* of change is governed by the accident of the parents' politics.

Maccoby presents one other analysis which illuminates the conditions increasing conflicts over the influences of parents vs. other agencies such as friends. As earlier noted, in general, friends have less political influence on youth than do parents. Opposition is not experienced. However, when the influence of friends is examined for groups varying in the resentment of parental control, it is found that friends have a stronger influence in producing change among that group of youth who felt greater resentment.[49]

In Newcomb's earlier work on intra-family resemblance in attitude, another test of the influence of rebellion in producing political change from parent to child is available.[50] Scores on a questionnaire concerning conflict and antagonism with parents were correlated with differences in attitude between parents and children. The coefficients were uniformly low; no single one approximating .3.

In the early study by G. Allport on resemblance in voting between father and son, certain data illuminate the phenomenon of rebellion. As earlier noted, for the total group of Dartmouth undergraduates, presumably of conservative origins, 79% agreed in vote with their father. However, among the minority with *radical* scores on an ideological test, only 47% agreed in vote with their father, and among *conservatives* 84% agreed with father. Further, Allport shows that those who differ from their fathers show a more *consistent* ideological structure. While inferences as to the temporal ordering of these phenomena are not possible, it at least can be argued from these data, that rebellion seems to be rather generalized and thorough, rather than being a more symbolic or token rebellion against the party label of the father. The rebellion extends itself ideologically and has an intellectualized or coherent base.[51]

In our formulation, the need to rebel constitutes a special dynamic which may explain the extreme deviation of a small number of youth from the political views of their parents. The more general process is one in which parental influences do not conflict with subsequent experiences and the ultimate political orientation represents the contribution of all the agencies. Now, if we entertain the possibility that special dynamic forces may cause extreme deviation from parents, it is equally plausible that special dynamics might lead to extreme *adherence* to parental politics, despite other broadening experiences. The introduction of psychodynamic factors may well work in either direction. On the basis of this modified formulation, attenuation of parental influences via other experiences may be less than expected.

Himelhoch's study, cited earlier, while limited to the phenomenon of ethnocentrism, provides suggestive evidence for such a theory.[52] As a group, his Jewish subjects showed in general much less ethnocentrism than their parents as a result of the tolerant atmosphere of college. He then theorizes that students who are "self-rejecting," who have a need to exhibit excessive devotion so as to repress hostility to parents, or who cannot objectively criticize parents without suffering guilt will be unable to defect from their parents' ideology. As a test of this theory, for 34 of his subjects deviation from parents' ethnocentrism was correlated with score on authoritarianism, taken as an index of "self-rejection." The C was—.67; the more authoritarian, the less the deviation in ideology despite the uniform exposure to the liberalizing atmosphere of the college.

Notes

1. *Op. Cit.*, p. 142.
2. *Op. Cit.*, pp. 102, 103.
3. *Ibid.*, p. 104.
4. S. Lubell, *The Future of American Politics* (New York: Harper, 1951), pp. 28-33. By extension, change could come about through differential *death* rates occurring within given classes at given points in time.
5. A. De Grazia, *The Western Public, 1952 and Beyond* (Stanford: Stanford University Press, 1954), p. 24. The measure is, of course, not ideal since it only includes children of school age. Moreover, Lubell's theory could also demand such data for several points in time to see whether differential patterns are static or changing the political scene.
6. Thus, the Michigan study which documents familial genesis of party identification also documents shifting in the Roosevelt era and in the

1952 Eisenhower election, presumably a reflection of the potency of the candidate variable. *Op. Cit.*, Chap. VII. For another demonstration of the influence of a dramatic candidate in upsetting traditional ties, see H. Hyman and P. B. Sheatsley, "The Political Appeal of President Eisenhower," *Pub. Opin. Quart.*, 17, 1953-54, pp. 443-460.

7. See, Campbell, *et al.*, for a demonstration that the act of voting in the 1952 election had little to do with party identification. *Op. Cit.*, Chap. VII, Table 7.11, p. 108.

8. E. Maccoby, *et al.*, *Op. Cit.*, Table 1, p. 27.

9. We find little evidence in the literature on this particular hypothesis. However, Maccoby does present some very interesting findings on differential changes in ideology and party preference among young voters who for other reasons are shifting away from parental party traditions. She suggests possible consequences for political instability. *Op. Cit.*, especially pp. 30-31 and p. 36. Fay and Middleton provide some suggestive evidence by comparing the scores on 5 attitude scales of college students contrasted in their father's political party. None of the differences was significant suggesting that ideology may be inconsistent with the party loyalty transmitted. *Op. Cit.* However, in a parallel analysis, Stagner compares scores on "Fascist Attitudes" for subjects contrasted in parents' political party affiliation and finds significant differences. R. Stagner, "Fascist Attitudes: Their Determining Conditions," *J. Soc. Psychol.*, 7, 1936, pp. 447-448.

10. *Op. Cit.*, p. 27.

11. For empirical evidence on such a developmental process in the formation of tastes and opinions about mass media, see E. Friedson, "A Prerequisite for Participation in the Public Opinion Process," *Publ. Opin. Quart.*, 19, 1955, pp. 105-111.

12. *Op. Cit.*

13. *Op. Cit.*

14. *Op. Cit.*, Vol. II, p. 386.

15. Hill, *Op. Cit.*

16. R. Havighurst and H. Taba, *Adolescent Character and Personality* (New York: Wiley, 1949), p. 72, 240.

17. Meine, *Op. Cit.*

18. Burton, *Op. Cit.*, pp. 275-284.

19. The writer is indebted to Dr. and Mrs. John W. Riley for making certain unpublished materials available to him.

20. *Op. Cit.*, Chart XXXVII, p. 89.

21. *Op. Cit.*, p. 28.

22. Murphy, Murphy and Newcomb, *Op. Cit.*, p. 1003.

23. P. Salter West "The College Graduate in American Society" (unpublished Ph.D. dissertation, Columbia University, 1951), p. 150. With respect to politics, the greater dependency of the female may not merely be a matter of the lesser freedom permitted but also a reflec-

tion of a more basic value. Thus, Allport and Gillespie remark that the girls in their sample place greater emphasis on family values. *Op. Cit.,* p. 32 ff.

24. See, Fisher's summary, *Op. Cit.,* p. 89.
25. *Op. Cit.,* Appendix, p. 171.
26. M. Benney, A. Gray and R. Pear, *How People Vote* (London: Routledge, 1956), p. 108.
27. *Op. Cit.,* Chart XLVI, p. 103.
28. *Op. Cit.,* pp. 31-32.
29. *Op. Cit., Chart* XLII, p. 97.
30. *Ibid., Chart* LXVII, p. 135.
31. *Op. Cit.*
32. Adapted from H. Hartshorne, M. May and F. Shuttleworth, *Studies in the Nature of Character* ("Studies in the Organization of Character," III [New York: Macmillan, 1930]), p. 98, Table I.
33. *Ibid.,* p. 100, Table III.
34. The findings are taken from A. Kassof, "Status and Politics, A Study in the Communication of Political Values" (unpublished thesis, Rutgers University, 1952). These data were made available to the writer by Dr. John W. Riley whose generosity is acknowledged.
35. *Op. Cit.,* pp. 117-120. It should be clear to the reader that *no direct* measure of mobility is available and that absolute income level is used as an indicator, perhaps approximate, of intergenerational mobility.
36. *Op. Cit.,* pp. 33-36.
37. *Op. Cit., Chart* XXXIX, p. 91.
38. The apparent difference in findings is all the more fascinating when one considers two other facts. Elmira is predominantly Republican whereas Cambridge is predominantly Democratic, making it more surprising that the upward mobility should have greater effect in Cambridge. In addition, it has been well established that young people as a generation have been more Democratic (see below), again making it surprising that the differential findings have the pattern they do.
39. See, for example, the Michigan study in which the predominance of Democratic families is greater in the South than in other regions, *Op. Cit.,* pp. 98-100.
40. The magnitude of such movement into a new political atmosphere is attested by Census reports. Thus, for example, in the one year period, 1952-53, about 400,000 children under 18 years of age moved from non-farm areas to farms, and about 600,000 children moved from farms to non-farm areas. Similarly, during a period of about 3 years, 1950-53, for the total civilian population, there was a *net* movement out of the South into other regions of about half a million people. Obviously the *gross* number moving from one political atmosphere

to another was much greater than this net figure. See: Current Population Reports, Series P-20, #49, December 1, 1953 and Series P-25, #97, August 6, 1954.

41. P. West, *Op. Cit.,* p. 337. In the attitudinal realm, a classic study of this type is available. Sims and Patrick examine the attitude toward the Negro for Southern students in Southern colleges, Northern students in Northern colleges, and Northerners who went to Southern colleges. The latter group is the migrant or geographically mobile group and shows attitudes not like those of the group from which it originates, Northerners, but more like the group whose environment it shares. Further analysis by length of time in the South argues against the interpretation of selective entrance into the South of Northerners who are prejudiced. See V. Sims and J. Patrick, "Attitude Toward the Negro of Northern and Southern College Students," *J. Soc. Psychol.,* 7, 1936, pp. 192-204.

42. For the test, it is necessary to have the *two* contrasting cases. The Cambridge case alone would be indeterminate, because of the general finding of a drift toward Democratic party among the present generation of youth (see below). Thus, the finding by itself could either support our thesis or reflect this generational process.

43. *Op. Cit.,* p. 27.

44. *Op. Cit.,* p. 89.

45. *Op. Cit.,* pp. 31, 43.

46. The data are taken from Lazarsfeld, *Op. Cit.,* Chart XL, p. 95 and Maccoby, *Op. Cit.,* Table 4, p. 32. The Elmira data are presented for individuals of all ages, since the tabulation for the comparable young age group is not presented. Also the large size of the residual category is due to our collapsing a large number of categories originally presented including friends and co-workers who will not vote or whose vote intentions are not known.

47. See, for example, *Voting, Op. Cit.,* Chapter 6, on the political homogeneity of primary groups and the selection of such groups to accord with political predispositions.

48. *Op. Cit.,* p. 29. The index used involves the consolidation of information about the mother, father, traditional party tie and 1952 Presidential choice so that the numerical values will not parallel the earlier data exclusively on party tie.

49. *Ibid.,* Table 5, p. 34.

50. Murphy, Murphy, Newcomb, *Op. Cit.,* pp. 941-942.

51. *Op. Cit.,* see Maccoby's study for similar findings on the extended nature of the rebellion pattern.

52. *Op. Cit.*

Social Change
in the Wide Environment
and the Attenuation
of Parental Influence—
The Doctrine of Generations

6 Thus far we have been discussing specific experiences which might intervene in the lives of particular children —geographical or social mobility, harsh parental treatment and rebellion—with consequences for the child's political orientation. However, all children live not only in the environment of their family but in the wider environment. Insofar as the child's wide environment is much the same as the one confronted and then given meaning by his parents in ideological terms, we might expect the persistence of the parental pattern. However, since the world is ever changing, the child may grow in a larger environment quite different from that of his parents.[1] Thus his ideology formed in relation to physical and social realities may depart from that of his parents. The earlier discussion represents, so-to-speak, the child moving in a stable world. Now, by contrast, the child is stable but the world is moving.

Stated in these relatively neutral terms, the idea has plausibility and we shall present some evidence to this effect. In this form, a changing social environment is *another component— most extensive in character* in our model of learning of politics. However, when elevated to the level of a specific doctrine of *generations* and their central role in *politics,* the concepts suffer from considerable complexity and ambiguity, and the empirical demonstration of the doctrine is attended by great difficulty.

But prior to all such specifics, it can be asserted on the basis of all the foregoing evidence that the doctrine must be regarded in a modest light. The overwhelming resemblance between most parents and most children demonstrated in a variety of studies, despite the obvious fact that the world is ever-changing, patently argues against the general significance of the doctrine. It is this fact that leads us to locate the discussion of generations and the influence of social change in the section on individual differences, rather than in our earlier section on the generic process of learning of politics. The susceptibility to this influence may not be universal or may be constrained in many cases by other factors.

An immediate complexity is to be noted in the problem. The parents are also living through the same social changes as their children and this, unless disjunctive for one generation *but not* for the other, has no relevance to explaining the attenuation of parental influence. Obviously, implicit or explicit in the doctrine, is the assumption that the parents have already hardened their ideology on the basis of experience in earlier formative years, whereas the children are still in their formative period at the time they confront the changed world. The doctrine is confined to the influence of social change operating at an early point in development.

This disjunctive effect on the younger individual again seems plausible, but a moment's reflection indicates that in certain areas social change could well be disjunctive for *older* individuals and *not* for younger ones. Consider *economic* crises: obviously they impinge much more directly on the adult breadwinner who becomes unemployed than they do on the young child who is not in the labor market. Perhaps in the usual case it is the parent who is changed and the child remains unaware or protected from the larger changing and hostile world! Let us examine some data to this effect:

Jersild, *et al.,* studied 400 children, aged 5-12, in 1931-32, the low point of the depression.[2] Of these children 240 were from public schools and the parents of about one-third were either poor, unskilled workers or unemployed individuals. A contrasting group of 160 children of privileged families in private schools were also studied. Inquiry into the child's fears, dreams, wishes, pleasant and unpleasant memories was undertaken. The authors note that the children made little mention of economic or political conditions. Most paradoxical is the fact that the *wealthier* children were more prone to make mention of such conditions.

Lazarsfeld and Eisenberg, in a review of literature on unemployment and its psychological effects, remark that for children aged 6-14 there is no evidence of the effect of unemployment on sociopolitical attitudes. They infer that the lack of evidence is a product of the fact that such children are not old enough to have viewpoints on such subjects.[3] Needless to say, the influence of unemployment on the attitudes of adults has been well documented.[4]

Waldvogel conducted an inquiry into memories of early childhood.[5] Approximately 125 college students were asked to report all experiences up to the time of their 8th birthday of which they had any recollection. A reliability check conducted by a repetition of the experiment about one month later yielded satisfactory coefficients. The detailed data presented on the most commonly recalled memories include *no* reference to experiences that had any apparent political or economic content or implication.

Similarly, one might allude to the study, mentioned earlier, of Australian rural children. The authors remark that the class origins of the children had no effect prior to age twelve.[6]

It is also clear upon reflection that the political implications of such experiences with the larger environment are dependent on their formulation in terms of *ideological symbols*. Obviously, considerable sophistication is needed to see the connection between some environmental event and some more abstract political concept which is interpretive of the event. That young children would find this beyond their grasp is clear from at least one study.[7]

About 300 children from the 4th grade through high school were interviewed on their understanding of a variety of concepts such as democracy, radicalism, open shop, etc. The concept least heard of was "radicalism." Understanding correlated with age and grade in school .55 and .69 respectively. Thus a certain maturity is required for the translation of events into appropriate symbolic terms. Meltzer reports a high correlation between understanding and intelligence, suggesting again the need for sophistication, and the likelihood of individual differences in the translation of social events into ideological ammunition.

It is patent that the translation of events for the young child involves the mediation of adults so that the impact due to direct confrontation of reality is lessened. Normally, parents would still mold the child's view of the world—whether it is changing or unchanging—and thereby create some continuity in ideology. Social change mediated via *parents,* while characteristic of the United States is, of course, only one of many possible societal arrangements. There may be all sorts of parent surrogates and depending on the societal form, generational changes would be facilitated or hindered. Till now, we have treated parental mediation, in contrast with direct confrontation of the environment, as a factor attenuating social change. Bloch, the French historian, in contrasting parental mediation with a form of mediated social change characteristic of French peasant life sees the parents as a force for change in the next generation. In interpreting the conservatism of French agricultural techniques, the "peasant mentality shaped by centuries of experiences," Bloch remarks:

> "A society that could be completely molded by its immediately preceding period would have to have a structure so malleable as to be virtually invertebrate. It would also have to be a society in which communication between generations was conducted, so to speak, in 'Indian file'—the children having contact with their ancestors only through the mediation of their parents. Now, this is not true. It is not true even when the communication is purely oral. Take our villages, for example. Because working conditions keep the mother and father away almost all day, the young children are brought up chiefly by their grandparents. Consequently, with the molding of each new mind, there is a backward step, joining the most malleable to the most inflexible mentality, while skipping that generation which is the sponsor of change. There is small room for doubt that this is the source of that traditionalism inherent in so many peasant societies."[8]

In contrast with grandparents, Bloch sees parents as the "sponsor of change." In contrast with the offspring in a new environment, they appear rather as conservative influences. Yet, there may well be special conditions in which parents become unusually receptive to change precisely to facilitate the adjustment of their own children to a new and future world. Such conditions would perhaps apply to a radical and large-scale change in a society. Inkeles in discussing ideological differences among Russians brought up by parents living in a stable pre-Soviet era vs. those brought up by parents living through the Revolutionary period, advances this formulation. An approximate test is provided by asking a small group of Russian adults to retrospect about the way they were reared by their parents and to report on the way they reared their own children. Most striking is the "increased attention paid to political considerations in the education of one's children" corresponding to the way "the Soviet regime has progressively 'politicized' more and more areas of human activity."[9]

The considerations presented thus far are not to suggest that an *older* child would not be *directly* aware of harsh economic realities, but to demonstrate that certain aspects of social change may well have more consequences for adults than for children as a group. But, if the young child is insulated from certain aspects of the larger environment, and the older person is usually hardened already, the point at which such abrupt changes in the environment could have effects would be in the in-between years. Yet, our earlier data suggest that political party ties and ideology seem well formed by the first years in high school, and that the process of development is gradual. *Abrupt* changes in orientation around the time of adolescence due to larger events do not conform to the general pattern of our earlier findings. Perhaps the role of such events is small and works its way by slow degrees.

One other problem related to the concepts employed has to do with the ambiguity of the notion of generation. When we conceive of the "younger" vs. the "older" generation, we have in mind a concept of chronological age, and the implicit notion that being at a certain point in life and in a certain status has political consequences. When we conceive of the "lost generation" of World War I or of the generation of "Depression babies," we have in mind not a chronological concept, but the notion of a particular social environment—a *Zeitgeist* within which the individual developed. While the ambiguity can be resolved at the level of concepts, these two components are confounded in many empirical tests of the theory.[10] Thus, if we compare young vs. old *in the same calendar year,* we do not know which aspect of the "generational complex" is at work.

The contrasted groups grew up in different eras and different worlds, but they are also of different chronological ages. Even the meaning of the chronological age component of the "generational complex" is itself complex. We have the status implications of age plus the inevitable elements of aging such as infirmity, pessimism, etc., plus the fact that aging may simply mean the cumulative influence of *more* exposure to the *same* kind of environment.[11]

Another difficulty attends certain of the empirical studies of the problem. We earlier mentioned the possibility that *changing* patterns of differential birth rates among classes might be responsible for political change. In the comparison of different age groups in the *aggregate,* or the same age groups at different historical periods in the *aggregate,* any differences that appear to be generational may simply be *artifacts* of the different social composition of the groups. Similarly, longevity varies among different sub-groups. Comparisons of age groups in the aggregate may thus involve different types of individuals demographically. In principle, this can be solved by the introduction of certain controls or matchings, but it may often be neglected in practice.

Ideally, one should compare individuals of the same age at different calendar points and match them in social composition. Then one can isolate the influence of the larger environment, controlling the chronological component of generations. This approach is rarely found in the literature of quantitative empirical studies of political development.

A study that illustrates the virtues of such a design was conducted by Pressey.[12] Although it does not deal with the specific political variables under discussion, it provides support for our earlier remarks that the young are less responsive to the direct impact of social change. In 1923, about 1700 subjects ranging from children in grades 6 to 12 in Ohio schools to students in the four college years at Ohio State University were administered the Pressey X-O test. In 1943, 1700 subjects with the same age distributions in schools in Ohio and at Ohio State

University were administered the same instruments. Age and social characteristics are thus controlled and what is under scrutiny is the influence of the different eras these two generations had experienced. Considerable liberalization of opinion is demonstrated in the realm of morals, manners and taboos, but what is especially noteworthy is that the change is much more characteristic of the contrasted *college* generations than of the younger school children. Either the culture of the home has not changed much in two decades in contrast with the changes in the wider world—or more likedly the younger child is not yet responsive to the impact of social change and is insulated from it by his home environment.

In most studies of different age groups or generations, a reasonable assumption would be that all three processes are at work. The old are themselves changing from what they were under the impact of aging and cumulative experience; the young are molded by a different *Zeitgeist* and in part are reflecting their temporary status as young people who are less exposed to the ravages of time or the influences of cumulative experience with the same environment.[13]

One other prefatory note is in order. Granted that a central factor in explaining some of the differences between generations is the factor of social change—the *Zeitgeist*—one is left with the imponderable question of *what element* in the vast complex of changing conditions is responsible for differing political orientations. Writings in this area tend to emphasize the dramatic aspects of change—crises like war and depression or the rise of a new and dramatic political figure. The influence of such factors would be somewhat reminiscent of that process of attitude formation which, following the schema elaborated by Allport, we described as "trauma." But such a process does not seem central to the *general* empirical findings earlier presented. Moreover, if we ask in what respects the environment of young people in the United States differs from that of their parents, we can immediately point to many factors not subsumed under the dramatic. Most obvious is the increase in years of formal education in this generation plus qualitative changes in the curriculum and the significance of these should not be neglected. To illustrate the change some current estimates of the formal schooling of different age groups based on a national probability sample of about 5,000 cases in 1954 are presented in Table 20.[14]

Table 20. Variations in Formal Education Among the Generations in the United States (Sample Survey Data— 1954)

	PER CENT OF GROUP AGED				
	21-29	30-39	40-49	50-59	60 or over
College	22	20	18	16	10
High School	64	56	44	34	26
Grade School	14	24	38	50	64

We have already shown the high correlation of education with political orientation and authoritarian trends. A high correlation can also be documented for political participation. We shall have opportunity later to document again the importance of this variable. Moreover, as earlier noted, two major agencies of socialization for the child are his teacher and school associates, and increased schooling provides additional opportunity for these agencies to operate. Consequently, generational differences in political behavior may well reflect educational changes.

Let us turn to some data in the three political areas under study, bearing in mind these many complexities and difficulties.

Authoritarianism and Generations

Remmers' surveys, presented earlier, documented the fact that the children of different social groupings show patterns of manifest authoritarianism that correspond to the adult patterns within their social groupings. However, it can also be documented from the national survey conducted by Stouffer that the magnitude of tolerance for the rights of socialists, atheists, suspected Communists, admitted Communists, and for nonconformists in general, certainly a major dimension of democratic vs. authoritarian tendencies, varies with the generation of the adult person. Among adults, there is a steady decline in tolerance from the age group in their twenties up to the age group in their sixties. The data reproduced from Stouffer's work are presented in Table 21.[15]

Table 21. The Position of Different Generations On Stouffer Scale of Tolerance for Nonconformity

Generations	Less Tolerant	In-Between	More Tolerant	N
21 to 29	10%	43%	47%	528
30 to 39	11	46	43	682
40 to 49	15	48	37	615
50 to 59	18	51	31	426
60 and over	21	61	18	517

Stouffer then confronts the dilemma already described. Young people are more tolerant, but if tolerance is the sheer product of youth, and not education, perhaps they will be as intolerant as their parents when they become old. The answer is provided by another analysis he makes; the tolerance of different age groups is examined within separate educational levels. Within *every age* group, the educated are found to be more tolerant. It thus appears that even when the present generation ages, they will be more tolerant than their parents were. However, the detailed data also establish the *independent* influence of aging. Old people are still more intolerant than young people, even when matched in education. More dramatic is the fact that the *differences* in tolerance among educational levels decline with age. With aging, all educational groups converge in their authoritarianism. As Stouffer puts it for a youth of today: "Although he is likely to be more tolerant when he reaches 60 than were his own parents at 60, he may at the same time be less tolerant than he was in his own younger days."[16]

In a subsequent analysis Stouffer seeks to find the intervening variables that underlie these generational differences in tolerance. He thus asks what psychological factors might derive from the exposure of youth to more education, which in turn would account for their tolerance; similarly what factors might accompany the lesser education, different environment and aging process in the old which relate to their intolerance. He is able to establish the presence of several such psychological factors, differently distributed among old and young, and to demonstrate their correlation with intolerance scores. Thus, pessimism is present in the less educated, accompanies aging, and goes with intolerance. Rigidity and authoritarian and conformist views accompany lack of education and are more present among the old, presumably accounting for their intolerance. Thus, it is Stouffer's view that some *erosion* of the greater tolerance of the present younger generation will occur with their aging and the decline of optimism. However, the lesser rigidity, authoritarianism and conformity with respect to child rearing he regards as a function of modern education and the *Zeitgeist*. Thus, he sees the tolerance of the current generation maintained to some degree despite the inroads of aging.

All of this analysis is predicated on the assumption of the *continuity* of the social changes that have occurred. External forces might move the current generation in either direction—closer to their parents or further away. Stouffer nowhere suggests the prospect for the *next* adult generation, the children of today. The pattern of education may well have become stabilized by now. Future unknowns in the environment must be reckoned with. However, there is a danger that the *reader* might extrapolate from the progressive pattern observed in the data for each group, and argue that those in their teens would be even more tolerant than those now in their twenties. The Remmers' data presented earlier constitute the next younger cohort, and the comparability of many of the questions in these surveys provides opportunity for an empirical solution. While it is not possible to make the complete analysis appropriate to the problem, inspection of these teen-age data suggests that tolerance has leveled off. Whether this is the product of the stabilization of the environment and the educational process or the emergence of counter-forces to tolerance cannot be determined.

Hinshaw by secondary analysis of a large number of questions asked of national samples by the American Institute of Public Opinion during 1937-43 finds evidence that confirms Stouffer.[17] The samples were broken down into three age groups, 18-30, 31-47, and

48 or older, and among the questions examined were five on civil liberties for radicals. Although the differences are not large, the young are significantly more tolerant.

So far we have treated the influence of generations in attenuating parental transmission of *manifest* authoritarian trends. But, what of *implicit* authoritarianism? It should immediately be noted that some of the intervening variables which Stouffer isolated in an attempt to interpret the *manifest* level of authoritarianism are the very kind of items which form part of the domain that has been regarded as implicit authoritarianism, and their exact wording is most close to items in the original F-scale. Stouffer's findings that these results vary independently with age and with education establish generational differences in implicit authoritarianism; such differences being in part a function of sheer aging independent of education and in part a function of the different education and larger environment of the young.

Kornhauser's study among automobile workers generally confirms Stouffer's findings, but also exhibits certain special departures. The better educated workers show less authoritarian attitudes (short form of the "F" scale) at each age level. Age goes with increased authoritarianism when workers over 40 are contrasted with those under 40, but only among those with *higher* education. Thus while both variables have independent influences on authoritarianism, in agreement with Stouffer's findings, it should be noted that the variable of age only has effect under specified conditions. It is as if the undereducated are already relatively so authoritarian that aging cannot produce any further deterioration.[18]

We turn to another inquiry for a more detailed treatment. In a survey conducted by Mackinnon and Centers, of a quota sample of 460 people in the city of Los Angeles, similar findings are documented for that dimension of authoritarianism that we have labeled "implicit."[19] A modified F-scale was used and it was established that authoritarianism reached a peak in the oldest age group. However, certain more subtle findings of this study are especially relevant to our discussion. These writers find in confirmation of Janowitz and Marvick, Stouffer, Remmers, and others that the lower classes exhibit more authoritarianism than do the higher classes. However, when they then examine the *developmental* aspects of authoritarianism with increasing age, *for separate economic classes,* they observe that the disparity between classes is reduced with age.

The older group despite upper class status moves in viewpoint toward the authoritarianism of the lower classes, which has all along been relatively authoritarian. The specification of the effect of aging parallels Kornhauser's finding. Here again it is as if deterioration can only occur in the one instance. In other words, the impact of the generation variable is toward obliteration of class differences in authoritarianism. Whether this is a product of the educational component or some other component of social change between generations is not established. The writers themselves argue for the factor of a *changing perspective* on the world as the individual ages. This latter component of the generational complex is supported by one feature of the data. The least authoritarian sub-group is the non-manual class in the *Thirties,* rather than the youngest individuals who would be more educated. This seems to correspond to the zenith of opportunity, prior to the stabilization or possible decline of opportunity and gratification with further aging.

One inquiry provides direct evidence on the influence of formal education in modifying implicit authoritarianism.[20] A large scale program of research on the role of higher education in the development of personality has been in progress at Vassar College for the past four years under the direction of Nevitt Sanford. We may conceive of college experience as involving a variety of agencies of socialization in addition to exposure to didactic material. One class of girls has now been tested both upon entrance into college and again during their Senior Year. Scores on the F scale are considerably lowered after four years of college residence.

Political Orientation and Generations

We shall first present data on attitudes as an index of political orientation.

A first and excellent source of evidence on generation differences in orientation are the studies of intra-family correlations in attitude. If instead of examining *resemblances* among family members by correlational methods, the *mean* score of the generation of children is compared with the *mean* score of the older generation of parents, a test of generational differences is obtained. Moreover, such a test based on members of the same families, by definition, controls certain social characteristics in the comparison of the two generations in a way that is not possible in the study of *unrelated* individuals from different generations. In addition, one can observe quite *directly* the attenuation of parental influence, most appropriate to our present discussion.

Such findings for a number of the studies of intra-family attitudes are summarized by Fisher.[21] Perhaps, the most important conclusion is that no simple hypothesis conforms to the subtleties of the data. True it is that the findings, in general, show a lesser conservatism among the children. Thus, Peterson obtained more liberal scores for children than for their parents. Newcomb and Svehla obtained more liberal (pro-Communist) scores for their child generation, but they also show that within sub-groups in given strata the findings may reverse themselves. Particularly, among lower occupational levels, fathers on occasion were less conservative than their children. Moreover, some of the differences are small or inconsistent.

In the studies of parents vs. children, the influence of aging is confounded with generational differences, although social characteristics are controlled. A unique longitudinal study by Nelson provides evidence on the role of aging apart from classic generational variables.[22] About 4000 college students at 18 colleges were tested on a conservatism-radicalism scale in 1936. After a lapse of 14 years, 900 former students were empanelled and retested. A variety of measures established that the mortality from the original sample of 4000 was probably not a source of bias. Comparisons of the 1936 and 1950 mean scores for the 900 subjects provide evidence that despite aging there is a small shift in the direction of greater *liberalism*. If turnover of individual cases is examined, the predominant pattern of shifting is still toward liberalism. It should be noted, however, that the component of aging, unlike the other studies cited, is merely from young adult status to perhaps age 35. By an ingenious comparison between the 1936 scores and scores of a new generation of 1950 college students, matched in certain respects, Nelson finds that the 1950 generation is also more liberal than the 1936 college students. He thus infers that aging *per se* is not the determinant of changing political orientation, but rather cumulative experience with the environment and the social changes that occurred between 1936 and 1950. The conclusion is therefore what might be labelled a modified generational theory, namely, that experience of social change, subsequent to the formative years, is operative. While Nelson establishes that this variable has relevance, other data establish that its contribution to political orientation is small. Sub-groups from the different colleges and individuals show a remarkable tendency to maintain their *relative* position of liberalism or conservatism despite their aging by 14 years and their exposure to the variety of intervening experiences.

By an ingenious secondary analysis of survey data from the American Institute of Public Opinion, Toch provides evidence on generational differences in political orientation.[23] Since such surveys are available over a 15 year period, age groups can be compared for two somewhat different eras, an earlier one beginning 1938 and a later era ending 1952. Thus, as earlier noted, comparisons of individuals of the *same* age at different points in time controls aging *per se* and tests the influence of the *Zeitgeist* on attitude development. By contrast, the influence of aging, apart from *Zeitgeist,* is established when the functional relationship between age and attitude is invariant no matter what the time period, or does not vary in the direction predictable from the changing ethos of the different eras. Measures of political conservatism examined in this fashion yield no evidence in support of a generational theory but do clearly document the fact that the aging process itself, setting in about age 50, produces increased conservatism.

In Centers' *national* inquiry in 1945 into class consciousness among a sample of white males, data are provided which bear on the relation of political orientation to generations.[24] Incidental to this analysis, there is evidence relevant to the Newcomb finding of an inversion in the generational process for different classes. Centers' presents the scores on this conservative-radicalism scale for age groups 60 years of age or older down to the age group under 30, *separately for different classes.* Among the business, professional, and white collar group, there is a progressive increase in conservatism with age. However, among the manual workers, the influence of age is negligible; old and young alike rarely tend to show conservatism. Whatever variation in age occurs tends to establish that the middle-age group (40-49) is least conservative. The finding is much in accord with Newcomb's finding from intra-family data. Centers' own interpretation is close to the classic view of generations. He sees this age group as hit by the depression at the time when they had entered into the labor force and were beginning to advance their careers, the consequences being "an embittered out-look born of depression and lean years."

This inquiry of Centers' dealth with a *national* sample in 1945 and the analysis above was confined to an age range above 20. In another study, Centers provides additional data on generations. This study, earlier examined in the discussion of the progressive socialization of the child into his class position with age, involved a sample of high school youth in one small Eastern city in 1947, mainly in the age group 16-18.[25] Centers titles his paper, *Children of the New Deal,* to emphasize the generational variable interpreted in terms of the very specialized environment of this age group: born as he writes "in depression, reared in unemployment and insecurity, constantly exposed to the ideology of three Roosevelt administrations, witnessing the dramatic victories of welfare legislation, T.V.A." In accordance with this environment, Centers notes that although these children mirror their class origins, what is striking is "the degree to which youth of all occupational parentages endorse collectivist views."[26]

No direct evidence is presented in support of this explanation. In addition, the finding itself is derived from sheer inspection of youth's marginal distribution on the ideology scale and does not include any direct comparison with adults. It appears plausible, however, and is in general conformity with his national data. Moreover, the significance of changed patterns of *education* on this particular ideological dimension, the factor which we regarded as central to explaining generation changes in authoritarianism, must be rejected for *Centers' data.* In *The Psychology of Social Classes* an analysis is presented of the influence of formal education on ideology, controlling occupation. Increases in education are associated with increased conservatism.[27]

Kornhauser presents comparisons of old and young automobile workers in political orientation, using a battery of items which tap "pro-labor political orientation."[28] The young workers are more pro-labor and this finding casts doubt on the classic type of generational theory which Centers employs. Kornhauser notes that it is the older members of the UAW who lived through the earlier era of unemployment, strikes, labor conflict and militant organization. Yet they are less pro-labor in orientation than the young whose development involved none of these experiences. Kornhauser rather emphasizes the influence of education in liberalizing the young, and the possible changes in status and perpective with progressive aging.

In Hinshaw's secondary analysis of national survey data, age differences in political orientations are presented for a number of attitude areas.[29] On social welfare questions, the differences are non-significant and on government ownership and regulations, the differences are negligible. On labor relations, the young are somewhat more liberal and on support of Roosevelt they are more favorable.

In the Helfant inquiry into intra-family agreement in attitude, some additional negative evidence is provided on the influence of age on political orientation.[30]. Since exact ages of parents were reported, Lorge and Helfant computed the correlations for the 163 parents between chronological age and attitude separately for each of the three attitudes studied and for each sex. None of the six coefficients was significantly greater than zero.

One study remains to be cited where age differences in political orientation are non-significant. Pollak by secondary analysis of Gallup, Roper and NORC data prior to 1943 finds 11 questions dealing with public ownership where age breaks between the young (40 or 45 or less) vs. the old (over 40 or 45) were provided.[31] The universes varied from national to local in character. None of the differences was significant, and conservatism characterized a majority of both age groups.

We turn now to party affiliation and voting behavior as an index of political orientation.

In the Maccoby study of a sample of youth in Cambridge, Mass., the shift of children from the political affiliation of their parents is examined as a function of formal education. Considerable evidence has been presented that this factor is central in accounting for many of the generation differences, and Maccoby's findings provide further confirmation. It is established that among "the college graduates in the sample, 58% changed to some degree from the political position of their parents, while only 28% of those who did not graduate from high school did so." The finding cannot be disputed on grounds that class or mobility is confounded—in that higher education would imply a certain class position or class aspiration: "At each class level, the better-educated young people change more." The direction of change is examined by Maccoby and it is shown that considerable shifts occur in the direction of *both* parties. However, the detailed pattern is of some interest. At the lower educational level, the shift is predominantly toward the Republican party; at the college level the shift is predominantly in the Democratic direction.[32]

The dynamics of this process are examined by Maccoby, *et al.* The hypothesis is advanced that education, by exposing the individual to a *variety of viewpoints* and a diversity of information, creates the basis for rational decisions about politics and thus attenuates the influence of such non-rational factors as family tradition. No strong evidence in support of this hypothesis is presented, although some suggestive findings are consistent with it.[33] The ideological structure of the well educated youth seems congruent with their party choice irrespective of which party is chosen, suggesting the formation of a viewpoint on intellectual grounds.

Other studies on the influence of college education on the young also demonstrate its significance for political change. A most significant distinction must be drawn, however, between studies such as Maccoby's where college education is simply a *formal rubric* covering a *heterogeneity* of educational institutions, and studies within a *specific* college, where in addition to the formal training, all subjects are exposed to a relatively *homogeneous philosophy or atmosphere.*

Thus, Newcomb's study seems to be in contradiction of the Maccoby finding. The essential drift among the students with increased exposure to education was toward radicalism. However, as Newcomb establishes in comparative studies of other college communities this pattern is particular to the Bennington community, and not general for exposure to higher education as such. Students in Williams College and Skidmore College did not show the same trend; there were slight drops in conservatism but the data are not progressive from year to year. More dramatic evidence, although not as comprehensive, is presented by Newcomb for a Catholic college. A portion of the student body was tested in the same year as in the case of the three other institutions. Here, by contrast, the "attitude climate" was relatively homogeneous but opposed in direction to the atmosphere found for Bennington.[34]

Inferential data on generations and political orientation as reflected in *party affiliation* are available from the Michigan study. As earlier noted, the respondents reported on their parents' party ties. On this basis, Campbell *et al.* report that younger individuals, those coming of age after 1928, have parents who were predominantly Democratic. By contrast, among those respondents who came of age prior to 1928 the party split among parents is only slightly in favor of the Democrats and this edge is contributed completely by the South.[35]

Thus, parents of a *more recent generation* had Democratic leanings and these data are not dependent on that aspect of generations having to do with physical *aging*. If we accept the validity of the report to the question, it should be noted that the respondents retrospected on their parents' politics, *at the time that they were growing up*. Thus, chronological age is presumably constant and they are presumably reporting on parents of a relatively young age. Yet, the young parents of an earlier era and generation were predominantly Republican, and the young parents of a later era or generation were predominantly Democratic.

More direct evidence on the generation process is provided by the same Michigan study. The respondents were asked to retrospect about the way they themselves had cast their *first* vote. Campbell, *et al.*, note that voters coming of age in elections beginning with 1932 voted predominantly Democratic.

A more refined analysis of generations is then provided in the Michigan study by the examination of *"delayed"* first votes by political era.[36] It is established that those individuals who did not cast their first vote at the time of their majority, but at some subsequent election, follow the same pattern observed for the first voters. In elections beginning with 1932 and running through 1948, the delayed first voters, just like the non-delayed, went predominantly to the Democratic party. This finding strengthens the likelihood that the earlier findings on first voters going Democratic is not a function of that generational component that we have labeled sheer *youth and aging.* The delayed voters are *chronologically* an older group; yet they behave the same way as the more youthful individuals. What must be at work is the atmosphere at the time of their arrival in politics, whose traces are carried along into subsequent stages of their life. The writers in conjecturing about the political atmosphere of that era give a central role to Roosevelt, although no direct evidence on his influence is presented.

The Elmira study also provides data on generation factors as they were manifested in the 1948 Presidential election. The analyses suggest that generation factors interact with more traditional sources of cleavage in political orientation. However, it should be noted that, dependent on what source of cleavage is examined, the effect of generation may vary. Thus, it is established that class differences in orientation are *heightened* in the younger age group.[37] Among older individuals, presumably introduced into politics in the pre-Roosevelt era, class origins make for about a 20 percent point difference in vote for the Republicans in 1948. Among young individuals, introduced into politics since the New Deal era, the effect of class is to make for almost a 40 percentage point difference. Thus, the social conditions which heightened class awareness in more recent times are reflected in greater class cleavages in vote among the young. One might restate the finding in still another fashion contrary to usual thinking about generations. The younger generation is not a uniform group in orientation.

Lest this appear to be a general law—in which the recent generations have heightened awareness of *all* their group loyalties as contrasted with the older generation—another finding in the Elmira study should be noted. The party vote of Protestants vs. Catholics is examined among different age groups. By contrast with the finding on class, the effect of youth is to *reduce* religious cleavages. Among older individuals, Protestants and Catholics differ by about 70 percentage points; among the young, the difference is less than 30 percentage points. Here, the effect presumably of the political atmosphere of the younger generation is to unify the group by the weakening of religious factors.[38]

The earlier panel study of voting, *The People's Choice,* confirms the Elmira finding on religious differences as they relate to political generations. Here again—for another community and another election, Erie County in 1940—religious differences have less effect among the younger age group.[39] While the interpretations advanced are plausible it should be noted for these analyses in Elmira and Erie County, that it is impossible to separate the influence of the generation components, political atmosphere vs. aging. But it can be said that the generation *complex* has these effects.

Comparative findings on the interaction of generation and class in determining vote are available for England. Benney, *et al.,* conducted a panel study during the General Election of 1950 on a sample of 950 respondents drawn from the electoral register of Greenwich.[40] The young (under 50) voted Labour, the old voted Conservative, and this holds when class is controlled. From the same data, it is clear, as in Elmira, that among the young, the influence of class on vote is much greater than among the old. Benney suggests that this differential effect cannot be due to aging and the growth of a conservative view. He suggests a generational difference in the exposure to given political parties. As he puts it, "A man of Mr. Churchill's age who had lived in Greenwich all his life would have reached middle age and have voted in 4 general elections before he ever had a chance to vote for a Labour candidate."

The report on the national study of college graduates, *They Went to College,* also analyzed the influence of generation on class cleavages in political orientation.[41] Since the finding is somewhat at variance with that of the Elmira study, it should be emphasized that the context of the reseach was quite different. This was a relatively homogeneous group—all college graduates—and they showed a strikingly high proportion of Republicans in contrast with more heterogeneous samplings of the national population. It should also be noted that the analysis dealt with traditional party affiliation as expressed in an off-year, 1947, rather than with a specific vote.

The most general finding is that Republican affiliation increases within this group directly with age. The analysts emphasize that the component at work cannot be established. It may be the influence of aging as such in changing a graduate toward greater conservatism, or it may be that the older graduates were initially influenced by the more Republican atmosphere of their youth. However, in contrast with the Elmira study wherein class cleavages in voting characterize the young, among college graduates income cleavages have *less* effect in the young group, despite the tendency of aging to produce greater *uniformity* of Republican point of view.

Kornhauser presents data on age differences in voting patterns in the 1952 Presidential election for UAW members, a group in which homogeneity in occupation is assured by definition.[42] Here again it is shown that the older vote more Republican, despite the uniformity of pro-Democratic forces impinging on all workers through common union norms and common occupation. It should, however, be noted that age and all other demographic determinants were relatively unimportant. In contrast with the national population, every sub-group studied was predominantly Democratic. The age differences do not seem explainable in terms of a generational doctrine, since, if anything, the old workers were probably those whose earlier work histories involved a more radical era.

We have presented a variety of studies which establish the influence of generations on political orientation and authoritarianism.[43] In some of these studies, it is possible to isolate which component of the complex is at work. In other studies, where such refinement is not possible, one can nevertheless establish the role of the total complex of factors.

These studies were introduced mainly to demonstrate one more factor attenuating parental influence, but some of these studies also bear on the larger problem of further changes in political behavior with age. While socialization is mainly a product of experiences within the formative years, these studies show that the individual is not then fixed in his politics for life. He may show further changes with cumulative experience in the large society or in a particular segment of that society. And as he ages his general viewpoint may change with consequences for his politics.

Notes

1. It should be noted that there could be great variation in the *magnitude* of social change between the worlds of parents and children, Thus, in some instances the world being relatively stable, the factor would not radically attenuate parental influence.
2. A. Jersild, F. Markey, C. Jersild, *Children's Fears, Dreams, Wishes, Daydreams, Likes, Dislikes, Pleasant and Unpleasant Memories,* Child Development Monog. #12, 1933.
3. P. Lazarsfeld and P. Eisenberg, "The Psychological Effects of Unemployment," *Psychol. Bull.,* 35, 1938, pp. 358-390.
4. See for example, E. Rundquist and R. Sletto, *Personality in the Depression; a Study in the Measurement of Attitudes* (Minneapolis: The U. of Minnesota Press, 1936); O. Hall, "Attitudes and Unemployed Men," *Arch. Psychol.,* 165, 1934.
5. S. Waldvogel, "Memory for Early Childhood," *Psychol. Monog.,* 62, #4, 1948.
6. Oeser and Emery, *Op. Cit.*
7. H. Meltzer, "Talkativeness about, in relation to knowledge of, Social Concepts in Children," *Ped. Sem.,* 33, 1926, pp. 497-507.
8. M. Bloch, *The Historian's Craft* (New York: Knopf, 1953), pp. 39-41. I am indebted to Prof. S. Diamond for bringing this reference to my attention.
9. A. Inkeles, "Social Change and Social Character: The Role of Parental Mediation," *J. Soc. Issues,* XI, #2, 1955, pp. 12-23. A similar design was employed by the Lynds in *Middletown* and is discussed below (see p. 124).
10. Thus, Mannheim in his essay on the problem states on two separate occasions that he *will ignore* one aspect of the problem, that of "aging." While it is possible to *ignore* such an aspect when one limits himself to a speculative or analytic discussion, ignoring the fact does not prevent its intrusion when one deals with empirical data. See K. Mannheim, "The Problem of Generations," in *Essays in the Sociology of Knowledge* (New York: Oxford University Press, 1952), Chapter VII, especially pp. 293. 296.
11. On occasion, the inference as to which factor is at work is fairly easy to make on the basis of sheer reflection. Thus, Cavan, *et al.,* document a marked decline in political participation (membership in organizations, attendance at meetings and offices held) and in interest in such paritcipation when groups ranging from age 60 to 90 plus are compared. The likelihood is great that this decline represents the component of physical aging with failing vitality and illness rather

than any earlier generational differences in participation. See, Cavan, Burgess, *et al., Personal Adjustment in Old Age* (Chicago: Science Research Associates, 1949), pp. 48-50.

12. S. Pressey, "Changes from 1923 to 1943 in the Attitudes of Public School and University Students," *J. Psychol.,* 21, 1946, pp. 173-188. See also his subsequent study which followed the process for the next decade up to 1953. S. Pressey and A. Jones, "1923-1953 and 20-60 Age Changes in Moral Codes, Anxieties and Interests, As Shown by the 'X-O Tests,'" *J. Psychol.,* 39-40, 1955, pp. 485-502.

13. For a critical treatment of the problem in the larger field of attitude measurement, see Murphy, Murphy, and Newcomb, *Op. Cit.,* pp. 919-929, 980-993. All sorts of possible designs can be elaborated to treat of this generational problem and the specific measure of social change. Each may resolve a given problem, but may have limitations in other respects. Thus, for example, one could use cultural artifacts as indices of attitudinal change. Then by trend data on changes in these artifacts one presumably measures changes which correspond to the *aggregate populations* living in different eras apart from factors of sheer aging. But what is confounded is possible changes in the age composition of the populations of the different eras, and if the time points are fairly close one may be dealing with a portion of the original population which has aged. For such an approach see Hornell Hart, "Changing Social Attitudes and Interests," in *Recent Social Trends in the United States,* 1933.

14. S. Stouffer, *Communism, Conformity and Civil Liberties* (New York: Doubleday, 1955), p. 92. The data are grouped into gross categories for our illustration purposes. (Unfortunately, the number of cases in each of the age groups is not reported.) Similar figures are reported for an earlier time period, 1940, by the Twentieth Century Fund. While not as striking, they show the great increase in formal education in the younger generations in the population. Thus, if one examines median years of schooling completed, beginning with the group 75 years of age or more, and going down the age structure to young adults, in their twenties, the increase is progressive, going from a median of 8.0 years to a median of 11.2 years. The proportion with some college approximately doubles over this same span from oldest to youngest generation. See *America's Needs and Resources* (New York: Twentieth Century Fund, 1947), p. 301.

15. *Op. Cit.,* p. 89.

16. *Ibid.,* p. 94.

17. R. P. Hinshaw, "The Relation of Information and Opinions to Age" (unpublished Ph.D. dissertation, Princeton University, 1944).

18. *Op. Cit.,* p. 169. It should be noted that the difficulty mentioned earlier that aggregates of individuals differing in age may well differ in social composition is probably operative here. Thus, for example,

while the sample is homogeneous in occupation, older automobile workers may well be of different ethnicity and ethnicity has effects on authoritarianism.

19. W. MacKinnon and R. Centers, "Authoritarianism and Urban Stratification," *Amer. J. Social.*, 61, 1955-56, pp. 610-620.

20. H. Webster, "Some Quantitative Results," *J. Soc. Issues*, 12, #4, 1956, p. 31.

21. S. Fisher, *Op. Cit.*, pp. 52-54 and especially Table 12. Himelhoch presents evidence that his subjects as a group were much less ethnocentric and authoritarian than the generation of parents. *Op. Cit.*

22. E. Nelson, "Persistence of Attitudes of College Students Fourteen Years Later," *Psychol. Monog.*, 68, #2, 1954.

23. H. Toch, "Attitudes of the 'Fifty Plus' Age Group: Preliminary Considerations toward a Longitudinal Survey," *Publ. Opin. Quart.*, 17, 1953, pp. 391-394.

24. R. Centers, *The Psychology of Social Classes* (Princeton: Princeton University Press, 1949), pp. 165-168, especially Table 69.

25. R. Centers, *Internat. J. Opin. Attit. Res.*, *Op. Cit.*

26. *Ibid.*, p. 325. This is a sub-scale dealing with government ownership and control essentially.

27. *Op. Cit.*, p. 164, Table 68.

28. *Op. Cit.*, pp. 216 ff.

29. *Op. Cit.*

30. I. Lorge and K. Helfant, "The Independence of Chronological Age and Socio-Political Attitude," *J. Abnorm. Soc. Psychol.*, 48, 1953, p. 598.

31. O. Pollak, "Conservatism in Later Maturity and Old Age," *Amer. Sociol. Rev.*, 8, 1943, pp. 175-179.

32. *Op. Cit.*, p. 37, Table 7. The contradiction with Centers' finding is difficult to resolve. Other studies to be presented now seem more in support of Maccoby, but the contradiction still remains. While sampling and technical considerations may enter, the writer is inclined to the view that the effect of education may well be specific to the conceptual aspect of orientation studied. Thus Centers treated "collectivism," Maccoby party affiliation; Newcomb still another dimension.

33. Campbell, *et al.*, remark in their discussion of party identification on the same possibility, that formal education inclines to greater rationality, subjects the individual to more information, perhaps makes him more selective with respect to specific candidates, and gives him greater competence in manipulating the complexities of split-ticketing. See their long footnote on p. 96, *The Voter Decides*, *Op. Cit.*

34. See T. Newcomb, "The Influence of Attitude Climate upon some Determinants of Information," *J. Abnorm. Soc. Psychol.*, 41, 1946, pp. 291-302.

35. *Op. Cit.,* p. 98.
36. *Ibid.,* pp. 103-104.
37. *Op. Cit.,* Chart XXII, p. 60.
38. *Ibid.,* p. 132.
39. *Op. Cit.,* Chart 7, p. 24.
40. *Op. Cit.,* p. 106.
41. *Op. Cit.,* pp. 115-116, and Chart 28.
42. *Op. Cit.,* p. 42.
43. The relation of generation to the dimension of *participation* has not been examined since the data are limited. Some evidence is provided by Benney, *Op. Cit.,* and there is evidence on age differences in non-voting, but the material is too limited to permit of adequate analysis. For an unusual analysis of national survey data on the relation of aging and various indices of political activity, see S. Pressey and R. Kuhlen, *Psychological Development Through the Life Span* (New York: Harpers, 1957), pp. 460-461.

Case Studies of
Political Behavior and
the Role of Idiosyncratic
Factors in Socialization

7 In our lengthy discussion of learning and socialization, we have suggested the operation of many factors. Nevertheless, our concern was with a general formulation. Even where we talked of individual differences, we still talked of factors that might well characterize a considerable number of individuals. All of this should be recognized as an oversimplification—admittedly a true picture, but one that glosses over the endless variations in human beings and their experiences which lead to endless numbers of different socialization processes into politics. The simplification was desirable in order to achieve some order and we used a lens that would not magnify the variations. But, if we so-to-speak increase the power of our microscope, we will now see the variety. And depending on how far we increase the power of our instruments, we get closer and closer to the idiosyncratic. Thus, for example, one may go halfway and argue that the process of socialization into politics does not follow one law for all individuals, but follows several laws for different sub-classes of individuals. Here, by contrast with our earlier discussion, one places the formulation by Riesman of the way in which politics shows different developmental cycles in the middle class as contrasted with the working class. Riesman conveys the point in the following way for the dimension of political participation.

> "In the middle class many people are radical or at least concerned about politics in their youth, and the campus offers opportunities for learning the political game; thereafter, one tends to become absorbed in business and professional life. In that life politics is unimportant and, if attended to, is dealt with as an agenda of the group into which one has moved— like giving to charity or belonging to professional associations. In the working class, if politics becomes an issue at all, it is a function of the group into which one has moved after leaving school, when one starts work and joins a union. In the union, however, politics tends not to be an other-directed status concern, but rather an experience-oriented class activity, where one encounters not only economic experiences but their direct link-up with politics through strikes, clashes with management, union canvassing, etc."[1]

Here one would also place studies establishing the fact that parental transmission of politics varies in character for different socioeconomic classes. A number of studies document such variations on our general model and, by induction, one could explore the multiple factors accounting for the specialized processes. Thus, for eample, in Newcomb's early study of parent-child resemblance in attitude, correlations computed separately by occupational level established that such transmission is strongest in the lowest classes.[2] The reasons are not established, however. The Lynds in their analyses also document various factors suggestive of class differences in political socialization. Thus, the lower class parents have less time to devote to their children due to obvious pressures of work, while the business class parents have more competing leisure time interests of their own. The net effect appears to be less opportunity for lower class parents to transmit their influences, but this goes contrary to the actual finding that Newcomb reports on parent-child resemblance. Another factor highlighted by the Lynds may explain why parental transmission might be less intense at higher class levels. Such mothers seem to be more attuned to cultural change and innovation and thus might be less prone to indoctrinate in the parental view.[3]

However, if one pushes the analysis to still more microscopic levels, the ideographic or idiosyncratic is revealed, and thus Riesman follows the formulation above with the remark about one of his subjects (Pizzeri): "Such considerations, however, useful as they may be in general, tell us little about the prospects for Pizzeri in particular."

A number of studies of political behavior are appropriate to this ultimate level of description and analysis. These are all studies somewhat clinical in approach, exploring the genesis of politics in a small number of individuals by methods of detailed interview and case study. One generalization may be drawn from these studies, and while it may appear obvious and negative in tone, its significance should not be underestimated. It is that no single formulation, even so complex and elaborate a formulation as earlier presented, will do justice to the range of individual processes. The phenomena treated in such studies, the reader will note, may be rather approximate to the political realm since the studies employing methods appropriate for our purposes are so few in number that we cannot be too particular. Let us illustrate some of the findings.

Iisager administered a questionnaire to a group of 76 men and women ranging in age from 17 to 35, resident at International People's College in Denmark.[4] The individuals were asked to report on the factors which influenced their level of *political interest.* A great variety of factors were reported with main emphasis going to the following: reading as a source of influence, parents and to a lesser degree friends as a source, and "reasoning" as an influence. Iisager, in addition, collected autobiographies and analysis of these data added to the above list of sources *another 36 contributing factors.* The most frequent pattern of influences among the subjects was a "mixed pattern" in which a variety of factors were present.

A number of other findings are reported. Interpersonal influences were found to be most important. Parallel to our earlier discussion, women reported more parental influence in the formation of their views. Adolescence was reported most frequently as the age at which political views were first formed. About one-third of the group reported subsequent changes from their initial views, attributing such changes mainly to dramatic incidents.

Murray and Morgan conducted an intensive clinical study of 11 Harvard undergraduates in 1941.[5] The inquiry in its coverage of social attitudes was concerned mainly with sentiments about World War II and relatively little with the usual range of political views. However, we shall regard this ideological realm as analogous to the area of *political orientation.* Generalizations are not emphasized; rather each case is presented in its entirety so as to convey the rich detail of the individual processes observed to lead to the particular orientation of each undergraduate toward the War. Their general finding demonstrates an intimate relation between personality structure and ideology, but granted this model, what must be emphasized is the great variety of developmental processes and the varied connections between aspects of personality and ideology.

Another study, very similar in design, was conducted at Swarthmore College, by V. V. French. Twenty women undergraduates and fifteen faculty members of both sexes were studied by intensive clinical means. Interview, personal history, various other personal documents, and such tests as the TAT and Study of Values were used to reveal processes underlying the formation of "philosophic-religious sentiments."[6] For the subjects as a group, the major generalization with respect to growth of ideology was that development began in early childhood due to a *variety* of experiences and proceeded gradually; in some instances, however, dramatic experiences were significant. Thus far, the findings seem much in accord with our earlier formulation. A variety of factors are shown to be of significance in development: parents and patterns within the family; exemplars outside of the family such as teachers, relatives, leading individuals; reading and formal educational work, etc. This complex of factors, however, is found to operate in terms of several contrasted processes of development which characterize sub-groups of subjects. Upon contrasting sub-groups in a rather unusual way, French reveals these processes. In an earlier preliminary inquiry, French had ordered her subjects by reference to how *highly organized* their sentiments were. This distinction does not involve the direction or content of the ideology, but is a *formal* dimension, i.e., atheists and religious individuals might both have in common highly organized sentiments.[7] When individuals of contrasted degrees of organization are examined, differences in developmental processes are observed. Thus, among the group with poorly organized sentiments, resemblance to parents is much greater. Similarly, the correlations between sentiments and other independent variables *within* "the family region" vary for the two groups. Only for those individuals with a high degree of organization, are sentiments correlated in any important way with factors "outside of the family region," e.g., college work and reading, non-family exemplars.

Breslaw conducted an intensive inquiry into the life histories of a group of 47 radicals and a group of 47 conservatives matched in many respects.[8] In general, no single factor or constellation of factors will account for the genesis of ideology in his subjects. Breslaw does find that when the *totality* of social influences were conservative or radical, a corresponding ideology is formed; and that the combination of experiences *early* in life are important. Since no single factor or simple pattern of factors is important, he therefore sees the process as highly variable in nature and dependent essentially on the number of influences of conservative or radical tone and on the sequential ordering of these in the life cycle.

In a series of papers, Queener reports findings of another study on the development of political orientation.[9] Long interviews on the development of internationalist-nationalist attitudes were held with 50 men, drawn mainly from the upper middle classes in New England and having a median age of 53. While the data are retrospective and limited to this one dimension of political orientation, the study is unusual in providing a test of a specific, well-formulated theory of attitude formation in addition to rich and concrete data on development.

Queener's subjects report, in accordance with our earlier discussion, *a variety of sources* which influenced their attitudes. Many of these sources are inter-personal, individuals acting as models for the child, who provide "cues" and who are at the same time "prestigious" for the child. Such individuals included family members and outsiders in positions within various prestigious institutions, churches, schools, and organizations. The concepts "prestige" and "cues" and their subsequent elaboration in the form of propositions leads Queener to predict *which* sources shall be the operative ones in socialization and to test this theory against his data. Herein lies the special virtues of the study.

His theory is that the individual imitates some *model* or individual who provides the *cues* for attitude formation. The model is not followed, however, unless he has *prestige,* which ultimately derives from the reward or punishment flowing from such behavior. To use Queener's terms, the "subjects' attitudes vary directly with the prestige of sources holding a given attitude and inversely with the non-prestige of those sources."[10]

Queener reports that his data follow without exception the requirements of the theory. "Mere *number* of attitude cues does not seem to form attitude. Mere exposure to an attitude does not even guarantee that it will *attenuate* the opposite attitude. In none of the histories did multitudes of persons or groups holding a given attitude form respondents' attitude *if their prestige was of an inferior grade* to that of even a few persons or groups holding counter views."[11] Queener notes the instance where several sources, providing different cues, may be equal in their prestige. Under such conditions, he observes that the more *proximate* source takes precedence.

In addition to this general formulation and the corresponding findings, data relevant to our discussion of the process of attitude formation are presented. Thus, Queener argues that attitudes formed in accordance with this model are usually discrete in character. By and large, the cues provided by the prestigious models are *specific* and the transfer is in turn specific. However, even with *concrete* cues, general constellations did develop in two areas, that of socio-political conceptualizing and that area having to do with the taking of life. In addition, a constellation may have been developed because the prestigious person who was imitated happened to hold the total constellation. Queener finds that the cues from the model are rarely presented to the child in didactic form. They are given in expressive form, through the practices of the model, and absorbed on this basis.

It is implied in the discussion that the family members are usually the prestigious individuals in early childhood. Then with time, love seems to be diluted by emerging sentiments of respect or lack of respect, and the older sources may be dropped as models. It is very prominent in the later histories of the subjects that certain kinds of behavior become evaluated in terms of the growth of social ideals: ". . . new prestige-cue sources impinge upon the individual from various societies so that acquired drives (social ideals) arise and the older sources begin to be reevaluated accordingly."

A set of clinical studies which document the dynamics of political development are those of Riesman and Glazer.[12] Here, the allusion is not to the primary theoretical work, *The Lonely Crowd,* but to the subsequent volume of detailed case studies which document the earlier theory. In these case studies, the mode of treatment is typically not a longitudinal or developmental treatment; rather it involves a structural analysis or interweaving of factors given in the contemporary field. However, the temporal ordering of the factors is oftentimes implicit, and these studies like the earlier ones cited demonstrate again the complexity of political behavior. One of the complexities revealed is that while political behavior is seen as related to character type, *content* of behavior is not predicted from character, but rather what Riesman and Glazer label "style" and "mood" of politics.[13] In part this implies the limitations of our schematization of politics; the contents we have labeled orientation, participation, and authoritarianism do not exhaust the domain of politics. In part, as Riesman reminds us, his character types relate to *"mechanisms* of conformity," and it is the accident of the historical situation which determines the *contents* towards which there is conformity. Nevertheless, this latter argument plus his other remarks on the tenuous relation of character and politics, suggest that personality factors do not flow in any obvious, simple way into specific forms of political behavior.[14]

The more specific features of the case material document the complexity even more. Riesman and his associates conducted their long interviews with about 180 respondents, so chosen that particular class, ethnic and social groups were represented. In general, contrasts observed show that the *development* of politics follows different processes dependent on the subcultural context, and further that the same phenomenon, e.g., apathy, involvement or participation, has different meanings and origins in these different groups. Yet, even within a most homogeneous social group and setting, individual differences are widespread, presumably representing ideographic processes. For example, 23 interviews were conducted in a most depressed area of East Harlem, New York, with Negro respondents, mainly women.[15] Earlier it was noted that the literature on the socialization of the Negro was almost bare of any discussion of politics. Here, Riesman fills in some of the gap, by documenting the fact that political inactivity is modal for the group and due to the fact that "the conditions of lower-class life do not train people in the motivations and techniques" necessary. In this setting, the activist was the exception, and for him it was necessary to invoke characterological factors.

A group of interviews with youth conducted in Bridgeport, Conn., provide a contrast. Here the social setting was that of a vocational school, catering to lower-class white individuals of various immigrant stocks. Five cases are reported, and it is noted that despite the common lower class positions, these show considerable variation in political patterns as a function presumably of temperament and ethnic differences and idiosyncratic experiences.[16] However, if one attempts to characterize the model pattern, this group also shows political indifference, low political competence, and low political affect, presumably arising from the social conditions characterizing their development.

A group of nine interviews with young people in a small village in Vermont provides dramatic findings showing that simple sub-cultural determinism is too crude a model. The village was chosen for social contrast as a site in which "inner-direction" as a character type would be found. The writers note that the adult group, by implication, the parents of these nine cases, are often not natives of the area. Parryville appears to be a "refuge for residual inner-directeds uncomfortable in other-directed settings."[17] Life in Parryville is described as one of "stringencies and scarcities" and for historical reasons the "elderly divide up the available social and political roles." The consequence for development is that the modal pattern observed among these *youth* is a "profile of apathy, of inhibited aims." Contrary to initial expectation, the political style of the inner-directed is *not* found among the *young!* The process may be summarized in Riesman's conclusion that for adults Parryville acts as one of the "inner-directed refuges where they can find contentment in grousing that others might find in carousing. The young, however, are unknowing captives of this process, deprived by parental 'opportunity' of their own range of future opportunity."[18]

Other youth interviews, conducted in varied school settings tapping other social groups enhance the picture of sub-cultural variation and corresponding complexity, idiosyncratic variation within the homogeneous social setting, and the unexpected and unpredicted finding. We shall not expand on the case material any further for our purposes.

A final set of case studies is reported by Smith, Bruner and White.[19] Building on the earlier inquiry by Murray and Morgan, intensive clinical analyses were conducted on 10 married, male subjects. The subjects were diverse in background characteristics but all were considerably above average in intelligence. Between 1945 and 1948, the subjects' opinions about Russia were explored in great detail and related to very elaborate data on individual development, family background, past personal history and to a long battery of measures of personality and intellectual capacities and functioning. The published account presents little direct evidence on the development of the subject's ideology. Rather, like the Riesman studies, the mode of treatment is that of a structural analysis or interweaving of personality and present-day ideology. However, the personality realm is, in turn, examined as a developmental phenomenon.

As in all the studies cited, the major finding noted and repeated throughout is that of "boundless individual variation."[20] Individuals differ in the exact processes by which their specific ideologies emerge. Nor is there any simple general relationship between content of ideology and a particular personality factor. Among the many explanations advanced for this lack of simple correspondence, Smith, *et al.,* stress a new and valuable point: "When one observes the compression of rich individual opinions into the 'yeas' and 'nays' of policy stand . . . one senses the relatively narrow range of alternatives by which individual opinion can express itself on public matters. It is no surprise to find a plenitude of different motives bringing men together in a common stand on policy. What strikes one forcibly, however, is the complexity of attempting to link deeper-lying motives with positions on such specific matters as the Truman Doctrine. In many ways, the policies upon which these men must take a stand have little directly to do with the substance of their opinions: the question always is whether a given policy proposal will serve as an adequate channel through which the more amorphous underlying opinions may be expressed."[21]

Yet, there is a congruence between personality and ideology. Recalling Riesman's formulation, the content of ideology is not predicted so much from personality—rather the ideological realm reflects in formal respects the more general conditions of capacity, temperament, and personality structure. Ideology often reflects differences in the "qualitative use of mind"; it often reflects whether thinking vs. feeling predominates in the individual; it often reflects the "prevailing mood tone." The *expressive* character of opinion is illustrated in many cases. Thus, one subject gifted with high intellectual capacities for abstraction revealed an articulate, well-organized, differentiated view of Russia; another subject generally resistant to abstraction characteristically avoided seeing broad ideological considerations when appraising Russia; another subject with attitudes toward Russia that were subtle, elaborate, but somewhat disorganized and overstated, exhibited more general temperamental and intellectual qualities of the same nature.

As previously noted, this suggests that our three dimensions of political behavior hardly exhaust the domain of political behavior. What is further suggested is that the goals of political behavior, e.g., authoritarian ends, liberal ends, etc., need supplementation by dimensions which will convey the "style of individual politics" or the cognitive aspects of ideology. Certainly, our prefatory remarks on the

CASE STUDIES OF POLITICAL BEHAVIOR

need for a systematic treatment of perceptual or cognitive and intellectual factors in political behavior are underscored again and again in this inquiry.

The studies of idiosyncratic factors in political development should not be regarded as obscuring or marring the general formulation earlier presented. Rather these studies enrich our knowledge and are a necessary antidote to the more general formulation. Intuitively, one would appraise as *invalid* a general formulation which did not need to introduce the idiosyncratic in a Psychology of Political Development. Individuals are socialized into politics on the basis of their experiences in given groups and environments, yes, but they are not victimized by such experience. They learn—they receive ideas—but they also actively judge the environment and select experience. Psychological analysis involving concepts from the area of perception and cognition and from the area of motivation and personality would be required to complete our treatment of the Psychology of Politics. The case studies presented remind us of the need for these two future undertakings.

Notes

1. D. Riesman, *Faces in the Crowd* (New Haven: Yale University Press, 1952), pp. 172-173.
2. Murphy, Murphy, and Newcomb, *Op. Cit.,* p. 1005.
3. *Op. Cit.,* pp. 143-149.
4. H. Iisager, "Factors Influencing the Formation and Change of Political and Religious Attitudes," *J. Soc. Psychol.,* 29, 1949, pp. 253-265.
5. H. Murray and C. Morgan, A. Clinical Study of Sentiments, I and II, *Genet, Psychol. Monog.,* 32, 1945, pp. 3-139, 153-311.
6. V. V. French, "The Structure of Sentiments, III, A Study of Philosophico-Religious Sentiments," *Journ. Personality,* 16, 1947-48, pp. 209-244.
7. The earlier study is reported in: "The Structure of Sentiments, II, A. Preliminary Study of Sentiments," *Journ. Personality,* 16, 1947-48, pp. 78-108. This distinction turns out to be most valuable for sys-

tematic treatment of the relation between personality factors and political orientation.

8. B. Breslaw, "The Development of a Socio-Economic Attitude," *Arch. Psychol.*, #226, 1938.
9. L. Queener, "The Development of Internationalist Attitudes, I. Hypotheses and Verifications," *J. Soc. Psychol.*, 29, 1949, pp. 221-235; II, "Attitude Cues and Prestige," pp. 237-252; III, "The Literature and a Point of View," 30, 1949, pp. 105-126.
10. *Ibid.*, I, p. 224.
11. *Ibid.*, I, p. 227 (italics ours).
12. D. Riesman in collaboration with N. Glazer, *Faces in the Crowd; Individual Studies in Character and Politics* (New Haven: Yale University Press, 1952).
13. D. Riesman, *et al., The Lonely Crowd* (New Haven: Yale University Press, 1950), Chap. VIII, and *Faces in the Crowd* (New Haven: Yale University Press, 1952), pp. 54-69.
14. It might be noted at this point that the other clinical studies also cite this same difficulty in drawing inferences from motivational constructs to *contents* of politics. See, for example, Queener, *Op. Cit.*
15. *Op. Cit.*, pp.1-120.
16. *Ibid.*, pp. 152-269.
17. *Ibid.*, p. 274.
18. *Ibid.*, p. 280.
19. M. B. Smith, J. Bruner, and R. White, *Opinions and Personality* (New York: Wiley, 1956).
20. *Ibid.*, p. 241.
21. *Ibid.*, p. 247

Conclusion

In this work, literature relevant to a general formulation of political behavior as a product of learning or socialization has been summarized. It should be noted that certain specialized writings which we have omitted could well be exploited for a definitive treatment of socialization into politics. Thus, for example, some inquiries into the development of the self have explored the growing sense of membership in a class or ethnic or national group.* Insofar as these memberships have been established as major sources of cleavage in adult politics, the systematic treatment of this literature would have been legitimate. This would, however, have led us away from our focus on political behavior to studies of the development of the myriad influences which ultimately affect political behavior. Our concern has been rather with a general formulation and the supporting evidence. The formulation was intended to remind us of a neglected problem and to provide a systematic framework for inquiry into this problem. The treatment or inventory of past and current knowledge relevant to the problem was made extended and detailed. Our aim was to show on what aspects of the problem there exists already definitive evidence, on what aspects knowledge is sketchy and inconsistent, and to suggest the wide variety of methods which are available to future investigators of these problems.

Note

* See, for example, C. B. Stendler, *Children of Brasstown* (Urbana: University of Illinois Press, 1949); H. Hyman, "The Psychology of Status," *Archives Psychol.* #269, 1942; K. Clark and M. Clark, "The Development of Consciousness of Self and the Emergence of Social Identification in Negro Preschool Children," *J. Soc. Psychol.,* 10, 1939, pp. 591-599; E. Hartley, M. Rosenbaum, and S. Schwartz, "Children's Perceptions of Ethnic Group Membership," *J. Psychol.,* 26, 1948, pp. 387-398; R. Horowitz. "Racial Aspects of Self-Identification in Nursery School Children," *J. Psychol.,* 7, 1939, pp. 91-99.

Index

Berelson, B., 61f., 69, 79, 81ff., 86f., 94f., 115ff.
Bloch, M., 100f., 118
Breslaw, B., 126, 133
Brickner, R., 5, 15
Brown, F., 23, 37, 43
Brown, J., 15
Bruner, J., 6, 13, 15, 130f., 133
Burgess, E., 118f.
Burton, W., 24, 37, 42, 93

Campbell, A., 16, 37, 57f., 92, 114f., 120
Cantril, H., 6, 15
Carlson, H., 5, 15
Casey, R., 14
Cavan, R., 118f.
Centers, R., 27f., 37, 48, 50, 107f., 110ff., 119f.
Chambers, W., 21, 36
Chapin, F., 65
Child, I., 18, 36
Christie, R., 37
Clark, K., 135
Clark, L., 3, 14
Clark, M., 135
Corman, B., 69

Davidson, H., 29, 37
Davis, A., 36
Degan, J., 5, 15
De Grazia, A., 73, 92
Diamond, S., 118
Dollard, J., 36
Dooley, L., 14
Duffy, E., 53, 67

Eberhart, J., 5, 14

Eisenberg, P., 98, 118
Eldersveld, S., 14
Ellison, C., 54, 67
Emery, F., 47, 50, 118
EMNID, 25, 42
Erikson, E., 5, 15
Eulau, H., 14

Fay, P., 60, 69, 93
Fearing, F., 14
Fisher, S., 52, 53, 63, 67, 70, 80, 93, 109, 120
Fortune Survey, 24, 37
Freidson, E., 68
French, V., 125, 132
Freud, S., 4, 14
Friedrich, J., 22
Frohner, R., 37

Gallup, G., 112
Gillespie, J., 6, 15, 51, 67, 93
Gilliland, A., 53, 67
Glazer, N., 128f.
Goddard, H., 22, 36
Gorer, G., 5, 15
Gray, A., 93
Gurin, G., 16, 37, 57
Guterman, N., 4, 14

Hall, G., 22, 36, 77
Hall, O., 118
Harrell, W., 5, 15
Harris, A., 54, 67
Hart, H., 119
Hartley, E., 135
Hartshorne, H., 84, 94
Havemann, E., 58, 68, 85, 117
Havighurst, R., 77, 93